CAMBRIDGE TEXTS IN THE
HISTORY OF PHILOSOPHY

ISAAC NEWTON
Philosophical Writings

CAMBRIDGE TEXTS IN THE HISTORY OF PHILOSOPHY

Series editors

KARL AMERIKS
Professor of Philosophy, University of Notre Dame

DESMOND M. CLARKE
Professor of Philosophy, University College Cork

The main objective of Cambridge Texts in the History of Philosophy is to expand the range, variety and quality of texts in the history of philosophy which are available in English. The series includes texts by familiar names (such as Descartes and Kant) and also by less well-known authors. Wherever possible, texts are published in complete and unabridged form, and translations are specially commissioned for the series. Each volume contains a critical introduction together with a guide to further reading and any necessary glossaries and textual apparatus. The volumes are designed for student use at undergraduate and postgraduate level and will be of interest not only to students of philosophy but also to a wider audience of readers in the history of science, the history of theology and the history of ideas.

For a list of titles published in the series, please see end of book.

ISAAC NEWTON

Philosophical Writings

EDITED BY
ANDREW JANIAK
Duke University

CAMBRIDGE
UNIVERSITY PRESS

CAMBRIDGE UNIVERSITY PRESS
Cambridge, New York, Melbourne, Madrid, Cape Town, Singapore, São Paulo, Delhi

Cambridge University Press
The Edinburgh Building, Cambridge CB2 8RU, UK

Published in the United States of America by Cambridge University Press, New York

www.cambridge.org
Information on this title: www.cambridge.org/9780521538480

First published 2004
Reprinted 2005

A catalogue record for this publication is available from the British Library

Library of Congress Cataloguing in Publication data
Newton, Isaac, Sir, 1642–1727.
[Selections. English. 2004]
Newton. philosophical writings / edited by Andrew Janiak.
p.   cm. – (Cambridge texts in the history of philosophy)
Includes bibliographical references and index.
ISBN 0 521 83122 9 – ISBN 0 521 53848 3 (pbk.)
1. Philosophy. I. Janiak, Andrew. II. Title. III. Series.
B1299.N32E5   2004   192 – dc22   2004045821

ISBN 978-0-521-83122-2 hardback
ISBN 978-0-521-53848-0 paperback

Transferred to digital printing 2009

Contents

Acknowledgments

For their extremely helpful comments on the Introduction, I would like to thank several colleagues and friends, especially Nico Bertoloni Meli, Des Clarke, Mary Domski, Christian Johnson, Tad Schmaltz, and Richard Stein. I learned most of what I know about Newton first from Bertoloni Meli and Michael Friedman, and later from George Smith; I am grateful for all their advice over the years. Christian Johnson produced an amended version of the A. R. and Marie Boas Hall translation of *De Gravitatione* with my assistance; I am grateful for his expert work on that difficult text. Since the time the volume was first proposed, through its final production, my editors at Cambridge, Des Clarke and Hilary Gaskin, have shown great patience and much wisdom.

One couldn't find a more supportive partner or a better interlocutor than Rebecca Stein, who always finds time amidst her myriad publishing projects to talk with me about mine. I'd like to dedicate this volume to my wonderful mom, Joan Saperstan, and to the memory of my dad, Chester Janiak (1944–96); I only wish he were here to see it.

Introduction

Natural Philosophy consists in discovering the frame and operations of Nature, and reducing them, as far as may be, to general Rules or Laws – establishing these rules by observations and experiments, and thence deducing the causes and effects of things.

– Isaac Newton[1]

Newton as natural philosopher

Newton's scientific influence permeates our culture. Forces are measured in newtons, we have "Newton's rings" and Newtonian fluids, we apply Newtonian mechanics in a remarkably wide range of cases, and the law of universal gravitation characterizes what is still considered to be a fundamental force. Indeed, the very idea that a force can be "fundamental," irreducible to any other force or phenomenon in nature, is largely due to Newton, and still has currency in the twenty-first century. Because of these achievements, Newton is regularly mentioned in the same breath with Copernicus and Galileo as a founder of modern science. Although Newton is rarely listed along with figures like Descartes or Spinoza as a founder of modern philosophy, and although he never wrote a treatise of the order of the *Meditations* or the *Ethics*, his influence on philosophy in

---

[1] Quoted by Richard Westfall, *Never at Rest* (Cambridge: Cambridge University Press, 1980), 632. This passage from Newton's "Scheme for establishing the Royal Society" represents a contribution to the debate between naturalists and mathematically minded philosophers in the Royal Society before Newton ascended to its Presidency. For a discussion, see Mordechai Feingold, "Mathematicians and Naturalists," in Jed Buchwald and I. Bernard Cohen (eds.), *Isaac Newton's Natural Philosophy* (Cambridge, MA: MIT Press, 2001).

the early modern period was nevertheless profound. Indeed, Newton was one of the great practitioners of what the early moderns called "natural philosophy."[2]

Fully understanding Newton means avoiding anachronistically substituting our conception of philosophy in the twenty-first century for what the early moderns understood by "natural philosophy." To be sure, the latter includes much that we now call "science," and yet it includes much else besides. Just as Newton painstakingly derived proposition after proposition concerning (say) the motion of bodies under certain conditions, he painstakingly went through draft after draft of his thoughts about (e.g.) the metaphysical status of space and time and God's relation to the "system of the world." This remains true despite the fact that his work on the former bequeathed to us a conception of science in which discussions of the latter play little if any role. Interpreting Newton solely as a "scientist" whose work spawned discussion by canonical philosophical figures ignores his contributions to the philosophical conversation in England and the Continent in his day. Newton was troubled by, and addressed, a range of issues that he considered to be philosophical in nature. These issues include the extent and underpinnings of our knowledge in physics; the ontological status of space and time; the relation between metaphysical and religious commitments on the one hand and empirical science on the other; and the proper characterization of God's creation of – and place within – the universe.

Thinking of Newton as a natural philosopher can also illuminate his intellectual influence on eighteenth-century philosophy, an influence that can hardly be overestimated and that spans the entire century, both in England and the Continent. The influence has at least two salient aspects. Newton's achievement in the *Opticks* and in the *Principia* was understood to be of such philosophical import that few philosophers in the eighteenth century remained silent on it. Most of the canonical philosophers in this period sought to interpret various of Newton's epistemic claims within the terms of their own systems, and many saw the coherence of their own views with those of Newton as a criterion of philosophical excellence.

---

[2] See Howard Stein, "Newton's Metaphysics," and Alan Gabbey, "Newton, Active Powers, and the Mechanical Philosophy," chs. 8 and 10, respectively, in I. Bernard Cohen and George Smith (eds.), *The Cambridge Companion to Newton* (Cambridge: Cambridge University Press, 2002), and Ernan McMullin, "The Impact of Newton's *Principia* on the Philosophy of Science," *Philosophy of Science* 68 (2001).

Early in the century, Berkeley grappled with Newton's work on the calculus in *The Analyst* and with his dynamics in *De Motu*, and he even discussed gravity, the paradigmatic Newtonian force, in his popular work *Three Dialogues between Hylas and Philonous* (1713). When Berkeley lists what philosophers take to be the so-called primary qualities of material bodies in the *Dialogues*, he remarkably adds "gravity" to the more familiar list of size, shape, motion, and solidity, thereby suggesting that the received view of material bodies had already changed before the second edition of the *Principia* had circulated widely. Hume interpreted Newtonian natural philosophy in an empiricist vein and noted some of its broader implications in his *Treatise of Human Nature* (1739) and *Enquiry Concerning Human Understanding* (1750). On the Continent, Kant attempted to forge a philosophically robust meditation between Leibnizian metaphysics and Newtonian natural philosophy, discussing Newtonian science at length in his *Metaphysical Foundations of Natural Science* (1786).

Newton's work also served as the impetus for the extremely influential correspondence between Leibniz and the Newtonian Samuel Clarke early in the century, a correspondence that proved significant even for thinkers writing toward the century's end. Unlike the *vis viva* controversy and other disputes between the Cartesians and the Leibnizians, which died out by the middle of the century, the debate between the Leibnizians and the Newtonians remained philosophically salient for decades, serving as the backdrop to Kant's treatment of space and time in the *Critique of Pure Reason* in 1781. Newton's work also spawned an immense commentarial literature in English, French, and Latin, including John Keill's *Introduction to Natural Philosophy* (1726), Henry Pemberton's *A View of Sir Isaac Newton's Philosophy* (1728), Voltaire's *Elements of the Philosophy of Newton* (1738), Emelie Du Châtelet's *Institutions of Physics* (1740), Willem s'Gravesande's *Mathematical Elements of Natural Philosophy* (1747), and Colin MacLaurin's *An Account of Sir Isaac Newton's Philosophical Discoveries* (1748). These and other commentaries were printed in various editions, were translated into various languages, and were often influential.

A second aspect of Newton's influence involves thinkers who attempted in one way or another to follow the Newtonian "method" in natural philosophy when treating issues and questions that Newton ignored. Euclidean geometry and its methods were seen as a fundamental epistemic model for much of seventeenth-century philosophy – Descartes' *Meditations* attempts to achieve a type of certainty he likens to that found in geometry, and Spinoza wrote his *Ethics* according to the "geometrical method." Propositions deduced from theorems in Euclidean geometry were seen as paradigm cases of knowledge. We might see Newton's work as providing eighteenth-century philosophy with one of its primary models, and with a series of epistemic exemplars as well. David Hume is perhaps clearest about this aspect of Newton's influence. His *Treatise* of 1739 has the sub-title: "An Attempt to Introduce the Experimental Method of Reasoning Into Moral Subjects," and there can be no doubt that he meant the method of the *Opticks* and the *Principia*. Indeed, as Hume's text makes abundantly clear, various eighteenth-century philosophers, including not only Hume in Scotland but Jean-Jacques Rousseau on the Continent, were taken to be, or attempted to become, "the Newton of the mind." For Hume, this meant following what he took to be Newton's empirical method by pro-viding the proper description of the relevant natural phenomena and then finding the most general principles that account for them. This method would allow us to achieve the highest level of knowledge attainable in the realm of what Hume calls "matters of fact."[3]

Despite the influence of Newton's "method" on eighteenth-century philosophy, it is obvious that the *Principia*'s greater impact on the eigh-teenth century is to have effected a separation between technical physics on the one hand, and philosophy on the other. In the hands of figures like Laplace and Lagrange, Newton's work led to the progressive develop-ment of Newtonian mechanics, which remained the canonical expression of our understanding of many natural phenomena long after Newton's influence in philosophy proper had ceased to be felt. And yet to achieve an understanding of how Newton himself understood natural philos-ophy, we must carefully bracket such historical developments. To cite Kuhn's understanding of the development of a science, although Newton provided physics with its paradigm, he himself worked largely within its pre-paradigmatic context, and the pre-paradigmatic state, according to Kuhn, is typically characterized by extensive epistemological debates and controversies over the "foundations" or "first principles" of the science.[4] Newton himself engages in precisely these discussions both in

---

[3] A proposition expressing a matter of fact cannot be known to be true without appeal to experience because, unlike in the case of "relations of ideas," the negation of the proposition is not contradictory. This distinction lives on, somewhat altered, in Kant's distinction between analytic and synthetic judgments.

[4] Thomas Kuhn, *The Structure of Scientific Revolutions*, 3rd edn. (Chicago: University of Chicago Press, 1996), 88.

his optical work and in the *Principia* itself: his discussion of hypotheses, of space and time, and of the proper rules guiding research in natural philosophy are each intended to loosen what Newton took to be the pernicious grip of Cartesian notions within natural philosophy. So Newton's scientific achievement was in part to have vanquished both Cartesian and Leibnizian physics; in the eighteenth century, and indeed much of the nineteenth, physics was largely a Newtonian enterprise. But this achievement, from Newton's own perspective, involved an extensive, life-long series of philosophical debates. To ignore this is perhaps to ignore how Newton himself understood natural philosophy and its themes. I discuss several of those themes in what follows.

Newton's career and correspondence

Isaac Newton was born into a rural middle-class family in Woolsthorpe, Lincolnshire in 1642, the year of Galileo's death. Newton's philosophical training and work began early in his intellectual career while he was an undergraduate at Trinity College, Cambridge in the early 1660s. The notebooks that survive from that period[5] indicate his wide-ranging interests in topics philosophical, along with a reasonably serious acquaintance with the great "moderns" of the day, including Robert Boyle, Hobbes, Gassendi, and especially Descartes. Later in his life, Newton corresponded directly with a number of significant figures in natural philosophy, including Boyle, Huygens, and Leibniz. Newton's primary works, of course, are *Philosophiae Naturalis Principia Mathematica* – or *Mathematical Principles of Natural Philosophy* – and the *Opticks*. Each went through three successive editions during Newton's lifetime, which he oversaw under the editorship of various colleagues.[6]

---

[5] See J. E. McGuire and Martin Tamny (eds.), *Certain Philosophical Questions: Newton's Trinity Notebook* (Cambridge: Cambridge University Press, 1983).

[6] The *Principia* first appeared in 1687, ran into its third edition in 1726, just before Newton's death, and was translated into English by Andrew Motte in 1729; the Motte translation – as modified by Florian Cajori in a 1934 edition – remained the standard until I. Bernard Cohen and Anne Whitman published their entirely new version in 1999 (selections in this volume are from this edition; see the Note on Texts and Translations below). It also appeared in 1759 in an influential French translation by Emilie du Châtelet, the famous French Newtonian; remarkably, her translation remains the standard in French to this day. The *Opticks* first appeared in 1704, ran into its third edition in 1721, and was translated into Latin in 1706 by Samuel Clarke, Newton's famous defender in the correspondence with Leibniz; the Clarke translation ensured the text's accessibility on the Continent.

In addition to his published works and unpublished manuscripts, Newton's correspondence was extensive. It is important to remember that in Newton's day, intellectual correspondence was not seen solely, or perhaps even primarily, as a private affair between two individuals. It was viewed in much less constrained terms as a type of text that had an important public dimension, not least because it served as the primary vehicle of communication for writers separated by what were then considered to be great distances. As the thousands of letters sent to and from the Royal Society in Newton's day testify, science and philosophy would have ceased without this means of communicating ideas, results, and questions. It was therefore not at all unusual for letters between famous writers to be published essentially unedited. The Leibniz-Clarke correspondence was published almost immediately after Leibniz's death in 1716, Newton's correspondence with Richard Bentley was published in the mid-eighteenth century, and several of the letters reprinted in this volume were published in various journals and academic forums – including the Royal Society's *Philosophical Transactions* – in the late seventeenth and early eighteenth century.

Early work in optics

Although Newton's correspondence with the Royal Society and its members began reasonably early in his career, it is crucial for understanding his mature conception of natural philosophy and his life-long aversion to intellectual controversy. Newton's early optical work, which cannot be included in this volume, provides a significant example. In February of 1671/2, an article appeared in the *Philosophical Transactions* with the title: "A Letter of Mr. Isaac Newton."[7] In this discussion, Newton attempts to distinguish the presentation of an empirically based scientific theory from the presentation of what he would later term "hypotheses" concerning the nature of some phenomena described by a theory.

---

[7] "A Letter of Mr. Isaac Newton, Professor of the Mathematics in the University of Cambridge; containing his New Theory about Light and Colors," *Philosophical Transactions of the Royal Society* 6 (Feb. 1671/2): 3075–87; reprinted in *Isaac Newton's Papers and Letters on Natural Philosophy*, ed. I. Bernard Cohen and Robert Schofield (Cambridge, MA: Harvard University Press, 1958). Newton's so-called second paper on light and colors, read at the Royal Society in 1675/6, is also reprinted in the edition by Cohen and Schofield. Cf. also *The Optical Papers of Isaac Newton*, vol. 1, ed. Alan Shapiro (Cambridge: Cambridge University Press, 1984).

Consider the structure of Newton's argument in this letter:[8]

(1) It is commonly assumed that the rays of sunlight are equally refrangible.

(2) A first experiment shows that when a beam of sunlight is allowed to enter a darkened room and to pass through a prism, the shape of the spectrum projected onto the opposite wall of the room is oblong.

(3) The assumption at (1) predicts that the shape of the spectrum should be circular.

(4) A possible explanation for this divergence is that the prism alters the sunlight by breaking it into smaller rays that bear differential refrangibility (hence an oblong rather than a circular spectrum results).

(5) A second experiment – the so-called *experimentum crucis* – involves the same experimental set-up as above, with a second prism placed so that the beam of sunlight, having passed through the first prism, then passes through the second. The spectrum remains oblong – that is, the second prism does not cancel the effect of the first prism.

(6) Since the second prism does not cancel the effect of the first prism, Newton concludes that the explanation at (4) should be rejected.

(7) Newton claims that since the explanation at (4) can be rejected because of the experiment at (5), and because the assumption at (1) predicts that the spectrum should be circular when in fact it is oblong, we should reject (1).

(8) Newton concludes from (7) that light rays are differentially refrangible.

(9) In the experiment involving the second prism noted at (5), the colors into which the sunlight is broken by the first prism retain their indexes of refraction after emerging from the second prism. So the differential refrangibility of the rays of light into which the sunlight is broken is correlated with the colors of those rays.

(10) Since we have concluded at (8) that rays of light are differentially refrangible "originally" – i.e. this is not due to the alteration of the light by a prism – we can conclude from (9) that sunlight is heterogeneous. That is, sunlight consists of constituent colored rays of light; colors do not result from modifications of sunlight.

---

[8] I follow the interpretation in A. I. Sabra, *Theories of Light from Descartes to Newton*, 2nd edn. (Cambridge: Cambridge University Press, 1981), 240ff.

The first problem Newton encountered in response to this argument is that what he calls his "theory" of light and colors was immediately misunderstood, at least from his point of view. Soon after Newton published his paper, Robert Hooke responded with a detailed letter to Henry Oldenburg, the Royal Society's secretary. From Hooke's perspective, Newton's "theory" or "hypothesis" does not principally concern the claims about differential refrangibility and heterogeneity; rather, the latter represent alleged properties of the phenomena that must be saved by a theory or hypothesis.[9] So Hooke searches Newton's paper for such a hypothesis and finds the notion, mentioned briefly by Newton, that light is a "body."[10] Hooke takes his debate with Newton to hinge on whether light consists of particles, as he thinks Newton maintains, or of waves, as Hooke alleges.

Hooke was not alone in his interpretation. In a letter to Huygens explaining Newton's theory of light, Leibniz writes that Newton takes light to be a "body" propelled from the sun to the earth which, according to Leibniz, Newton takes to explain both the differential refrangibility of rays of light and the phenomena of colors.[11]

So for Newton's interlocutors, a scientific theory or hypothesis is, broadly speaking, a conception of the nature of some phenomenon; it is a conception of what the phenomenon is. One accounts for the relevant empirical data – one saves the phenomena – precisely by describing this nature. This does not entail that Hooke or others took the saving of the phenomena in this sense to determine which hypothesis about the nature of light is correct; on the contrary, Hooke's principal point is that his theory

---

[9] That Hooke does not think of these issues as forming an essential part of Newton's theory is clear for two reasons: (1) he is not concerned to reject the claim about differential refrangibility, but is concerned to reject Newton's theory; and (2) he takes his own hypothesis to be capable of accounting for both the fact about refrangibility and the fact, if it is a fact, about heterogeneity. See Hooke to Oldenburg, 15 Feb. 1671/2, in *The Correspondence of Isaac Newton*, ed. Herbert Turnbull, John Scott, A. R. Hall, and Laura Tilling (Cambridge: Cambridge University Press, 1959–77), vol. 1: 112 on the former point, and vol. 1: 113–14 on the latter.

[10] See Hooke to Oldenburg, 15 Feb. 1671/2, in *Correspondence of Isaac Newton*, vol. 1: 113. In recounting Newton's theory, Hooke does mention the points about refrangibility and heterogeneity, but he thinks that Newton's "first proposition" is "that light is a body" and that differently colored rays of light are in fact "several sorts of bodies." I take this to represent Hooke's interpretation of how Newton can account for the data with the theory that light consists of particles.

[11] In *Oeuvres complètes de Christiaan Huygens*, ed. Johan Adriaan Vollgraff (The Hague: Nijhoff, 1888–1950), vol. 10: 602. Ignatius Pardies, another of Newton's interlocutors, similarly found it difficult to differentiate the claim about the corporeal nature of light from Newton's ideas concerning refrangibility and heterogeneity. See his two letters to the Royal Society concerning Newton's work, both of which are reprinted in *Isaac Newton's Papers and Letters*, ed. Cohen and Schofield; cf. the discussion of Pardies in Sabra, *Theories of Light*, 264–7.

saves the phenomena as well as Newton's does. The point is that from the perspective of Newton's interlocutors, it makes little sense to suggest that Newton's presentation of empirical data concerning the properties of light based on experiments with prisms could constitute a scientific theory, independent of some hypothesis concerning the nature of light.

After the extensive correspondence, and controversy, generated in response to Newton's early optical views and experiments, Newton often threatened to avoid engaging in mathematical and philosophical disputes altogether. He insisted to friends and colleagues that he found intellectual controversy unbearable. Fortunately for us, he never followed through with his threat to disengage from discussions in natural philosophy, and sent many important letters in his later years. One of his more important pieces of correspondence after the optics controversy was with the natural philosopher Robert Boyle in 1679 (Newton's letter was published for the first time in the mid-eighteenth century).[12] In his lengthy letter to Boyle, Newton presents his speculations concerning various types of what we would now call chemical interactions; many of these speculations bear similarities to passages that appeared years later in the queries to the *Opticks*. The letter is also famous for presenting one of Newton's early speculations concerning how gravity might be physically explained; it presents, among other things, a picture of what Newton would countenance as a viable explanation of gravity in physical terms. This issue became of paramount importance once the *Principia* appeared.

Newton's relation to Descartes

Recent scholarship has emphasized that when Newton published the *Principia* in 1687, Cartesianism remained the reigning view in natural philosophy and served as the backdrop for much important research. We now recognize that Newton intended his *Mathematical Principles of Natural Philosophy* specifically to replace Descartes' own *Principles of Philosophy*, which was first published in Amsterdam in 1644.[13] As Cotes's famous and

---

[12] The letter to Boyle first appeared in *The Works of the Honourable Robert Boyle*, ed. Thomas Birch (London, 1744), vol. 1: 70–4.

[13] In his library, Newton had a 1656 Amsterdam edition of Descartes' *Principles*, along with a 1664 London edition of the *Meditations*. On Newton's relation to Descartes and to Cartesianism, see the extensive treatment in the chapter "Newton and Descartes" in Alexandre Koyré, *Newtonian Studies* (Cambridge, MA: Harvard University Press, 1965), and the discussion in Howard Stein, "Newton's Metaphysics," in *The Cambridge Companion to Newton*.

influential preface to the second edition of the *Principia* indicates, in 1713 the primary competitor to Newton's natural philosophy remained Cartesian in spirit if not in letter. Despite the astonishing impact that Newton's work had on various fields, including of course what we would call philosophy proper, it would be anachronistic to conclude that Newtonianism had replaced its primary competitor, for Cartesianism's influence did not dissipate until some time after Newton's death in 1727.

As his own unpublished manuscript *De Gravitatione* indicates, Newton not only read Descartes's *Principles* carefully, he patiently attempted to refute many of the central notions in that text. *De Gravitatione* raises a number of controversial interpretive issues, including first and foremost the provenance of the text itself. No consensus has emerged as to the dating of the manuscript – which remained unpublished until 1962 – and there is insufficient evidence for that question to be answered as of now,[14] but two things remain clear: first, the text is an extended series of criticisms of Cartesian natural philosophy; and, second, it is significant for understanding Newton's thought, not least because it represents his most sustained philosophical discussion.

De Gravitatione helps to dispel the easily informed impression that Newton sought, in the Scholium to the *Principia*, to undermine a so-called Leibnizian relationalist conception of space and time, just as his defender, Samuel Clarke, would attempt to do years later in the correspondence of 1715–16. Although Leibniz did eventually express what became the canonical early modern formulation of relationalism concerning space and time, and although Newton and Clarke were highly skeptical of such a view, it is especially misleading to read the *Principia* through the lens provided by the later controversy with the Leibnizians. Newton's extensive attempt in *De Gravitatione* to refute Descartes' broadly relationalist conception of space and time indicates that the Scholium should be read

---

[14] The text first appeared, in a transcription of the original Latin and an English translation, in *Unpublished Scientific Writings of Isaac Newton*, ed. A. R. Hall and Marie Boas Hall (Cambridge: Cambridge University Press, 1962). In the Halls' judgment, the text is juvenile and probably originates in the period from 1664 to 1668. Betty Jo Teeter Dobbs contends, in contrast, that the work is mature and was written in late 1684 or early 1685, while Newton was preparing the first edition of the *Principia*. See Dobbs, *The Janus Faces of Genius: The Role of Alchemy in Newton's Thought* (Cambridge: Cambridge University Press, 1991), 141–6, where she also reviews various alternative opinions on the matter. In a recent essay, Howard Stein raises several significant considerations concerning the question of dating – see "Newton's Metaphysics," 302 n. 39. Stein also discusses the broader significance of the text.

as providing a replacement for the Cartesian conception.[15] Newton had a Cartesian, and not a Leibnizian, opponent primarily in mind when he wrote his famous articulation of "absolutism" concerning space and time. It may be thought a measure of Newton's success against his Cartesian predecessors that history records a debate between the Leibnizians and the Newtonians as influencing every subsequent discussion of space and time in the eighteenth century.

Aspects of the *Principia*

Space and time

The discussion of space and time in the Scholium, and in the General Scholium, to the *Principia* provides the canonical formulation of so-called absolutism in the early modern period,[16] and the criticisms of Descartes in *De Gravitatione* illuminate this formulation. If one rejects a Cartesian view, defending in its place some type of "absolutism" concerning space and time – that is, if one contends that space and time exist independently of all objects and even of all possible relations among objects – there immediately arises at least one pressing question: what is the relation between God and space and time? Before God created the universe of objects and relations, did space and time nonetheless exist, and if so, what was God's relation to them?

As for the question of how to characterize God's relation to space and time – a question of considerable import in the early modern period – Newton presents, both in *De Gravitatione* and in the *Principia*, a complex and intriguing position. Roughly put, Newton's view has something like the following structure: (i) spatiality is a necessary affection of any being; (ii) God exists necessarily, so (iii) there is no time at which God fails to exist; and, therefore, (iv) space exists, and there is no time at which space fails to exist.[17] As we read in a now famous passage from *De Gravitatione*:

---

[15] This interpretation of Newton's *Principia* is presented by Howard Stein, "Newtonian Space-Time," in Robert Palter (ed.), *The Annus Mirabilis of Sir Isaac Newton 1666–1966* (Cambridge, MA: MIT Press, 1970).

[16] On Newton's absolutism, see Robert DiSalle, "Newton's Philosophical Analysis of Space and Time," ch. 1 in *The Cambridge Companion to Newton*.

[17] See the discussion in Stein, "Newton's Metaphysics." For further details concerning Newton's understanding of space, and for citations to relevant literature, see Andrew Janiak, "Space, Atoms, and Mathematical Divisibility in Newton," *Studies in History and Philosophy of Science* 31 (2000): 221–7.

> Space is an affection of a being just as a being. No being exists or can exist which is not related to space in some way. God is everywhere, created minds are somewhere, and body is in the space that it occupies; and whatever is neither everywhere nor anywhere does not exist. And hence it follows that space is an emanative effect of the first existing being, for if any being whatsoever is posited, space is posited . . . If ever space had not existed, God at that time would have been nowhere. (This volume pp. 25–6)

Notice that if Newton did not endorse the view that God created the universe, or if he were generally agnostic, his conception of space indicates that space would exist just in case any entity exists, for space is said to be an affection of any being whatever.

One intriguing implication of this view in *De Gravitatione* is that there is a sense in which God occupies space. In the *Principia*, Newton does not shy away from endorsing that implication explicitly, as a passage from the General Scholium indicates:

> He endures always and is present everywhere, and by existing always and everywhere he constitutes duration and space. Since each and every particle of space is *always*, and each and every indivisible moment of duration is *everywhere*, certainly the maker and lord of all things will not be *never* or *nowhere*. (This volume p. 91)

For Newton, space exists just in case God exists, and God is infinite both spatially and temporally speaking, so God exists everywhere throughout space at each moment of time. In this way, we can achieve a fuller understanding of Newton's view of space and time by reading *De Gravitatione* and the *Principia* in tandem.

Mathematical and physical treatments of force

Near the opening of the *Principia*, Newton contrasts what he calls the "mathematical" and the "physical" treatment of force.[18] In the definitions in Book I, after defining various sorts of motion and of force, and

---

[18] See the extensive discussion in I. Bernard Cohen's *The Newtonian Revolution* (Cambridge: Cambridge University Press, 1980), and the more recent interpretation in Andrew Janiak, "Newton and the Reality of Force," *Journal of the History of Philosophy* (forthcoming).

in particular after defining what he takes to be the various quantities of centripetal force, Newton writes of the concept of force as he employs it in general: "This concept is purely mathematical, for I am not now considering the physical causes and sites of these forces" [this volume p. 63]. Similarly, he describes his use of the term "impulse" by noting that he considers "not the species of forces and their physical qualities but their quantities and mathematical proportions, as I have explained in the definitions" [this volume p. 86]. So whereas a physical treatment of force describes, among other things, its "causes and qualities," a mathematical treatment eschews such a description, providing instead a characterization of its "quantities."

It is important to think of this Newtonian distinction as a technical one, that is, as a distinction that cannot be understood antecedent to its articulation in the text, despite the fact that it appears to be familiar. Newton's contrast is subject to misunderstanding precisely because it is easily conflated with various familiar contrasts. For instance, if the physical is identified with the "real," the mathematical might be identified with the "ideal," and mathematical models might be thought of as mere idealizations. In fact, Newton's mathematical account does involve certain idealizations. Consider, for instance, his caveat at the very end of the Definitions that open the *Principia*, just before he begins to discuss space and time in the Scholium:

> Further, it is in this same sense that I call attractions and impulses accelerative and motive. Moreover, I use interchangeably and indiscriminately words signifying attraction, impulse, or any sort of propensity toward a center, considering these forces not from a physical but only from a mathematical point of view. Therefore, let the reader beware of thinking that by words of this kind I am anywhere defining a species or mode of action or a physical cause or reason, or that I am attributing forces in a true and physical sense to centers (which are mathematical points) if I happen to say that centers attract or that centers have forces. (This volume p. 64)

This passage indicates an important idealization on Newton's part: material bodies are perfectly real, but their "centers" as he considers them are merely mathematical points. Although gravity is very nearly as the inverse square of the distance between the centers of material bodies, where the center is an idealization,[19] bodies themselves are not geometrical objects and so their centers are not in fact mathematical points. The actual center of a body has some extension. The question, then, is whether gravity in its mathematical treatment should be understood on the model of a material body, as a real entity, or on the model of a "center" of a material body, as a mathematical idealization.

To see that the "mathematical" treatment of gravity characterizes a real entity, consider how Newton describes a force's "physical" treatment, which serves as the relevant contrast class. The latter involves at least the following two elements, as indicated in Definition 8:

(1) A characterization of the "seat" of the force. For instance, does it involve an aether? A vortex, or some type of fluid? Etc.
(2) A characterization of the force's relation to other phenomena and forces; e.g. does the cause of gravity also cause other forces, such as magnetism?

Thus Newton's contention that gravity is a $1/r^2$ force represents what we would ordinarily consider to be a physical claim – one concerning, for instance, ordinary physical quantities such as the distance between two material bodies. But this is not a physical claim in the technical sense because it does not concern (1) or (2). So the mathematical treatment deals with perfectly ordinary physical quantities and relations, such as distances and masses, and not merely with mathematical entities and idealizations, such as mathematical points.

There are two distinctions here. On the one hand, we can distinguish entities into those that are mathematical, such as numbers and points, and those that are physical, such as distances and masses. On the other, we can distinguish our treatments of entities into mathematical and physical varieties. Hence a physical entity like a body or a force can be treated in two different ways: the words 'mathematical' and 'physical' modify the treatment of a perfectly real entity, not the entity itself.

We should acknowledge that the mathematical treatment of force in the *Principia*, which culminates in the derivation of the law of universal

[19] Newton, *The Principia: Mathematical Principles of Natural Philosophy*, ed. and trans. I. Bernard Cohen and Anne Whitman, with the assistance of Julia Budenz (Berkeley: University of California Press, 1999), 52. The work of George Smith indicates the significance of Newton's articulation of claims that are said to hold *quam proxime*: see especially "The Newtonian Style in Book II of the *Principia*," in Buchwald and Cohen (eds.), *Isaac Newton's Natural Philosophy*, and "The Methodology of the *Principia*," ch. 4 in *The Cambridge Companion to Newton*.

gravitation in Book III, also includes a startling unification of phenomena.[20] As part of his mathematical treatment, Newton contends, for instance, that the force that keeps the moon in its orbit, and that which accounts for the weight of bodies on earth, are the same force. Part of his reasoning is that two forces are identical in kind if their operation is governed by the same law; one might say that the applicability of the law serves as a criterion of identity. This unifies what were once called superlunary and sublunary phenomena, a unification that was obviously crucial for later research on gravitation.

Action at a distance

One of the most vexing issues raised by Newton's theory of gravity in the *Principia* is the question of action at a distance.[21] Any interpretation of Newton's own understanding of the import of his theory must acknowledge his discussion of the problem in a 1693 letter to Richard Bentley. The letter, reprinted in this volume, contains the following stark rejection of the notion:

> It is inconceivable that inanimate brute matter should, without the mediation of something else which is not material, operate upon and affect other matter without mutual contact . . . That gravity should be innate, inherent, and essential to matter, so that one body may act upon another at a distance through a vacuum, without the mediation of anything else, by and through which their action and force may be conveyed from one to another, is to me so great an absurdity that I believe no man who has in philosophical matters a competent faculty of thinking can ever fall into it. (This volume p. 102)

It appears that if accepting Newton's theory of gravity commits one to accepting action at a distance, Newton's own sense of what is an intelligible cause of motion would be violated.

Newton connected his understanding of the notion that all material bodies – or all bodies with mass – bear "gravity" as a property with the

---

[20] The "deduction" of the law of universal gravitation is extremely complex, and certainly cannot be explicated here; see Howard Stein, "'From the Phenomena of Motions to the Forces of Nature': Hypothesis or Deduction?" *Proceedings of the Philosophy of Science Association 1990* 2 (1991): 209–22, and William Harper, "Newton's Argument for Universal Gravitation," ch. 5 in *The Cambridge Companion to Newton*.

[21] For a classic treatment, see Mary Hesse, *Forces and Fields: The Concept of Action at a Distance in the History of Physics* (London: Nelson, 1961).

question of how to avoid invoking distant action when characterizing gravitational attraction. In his letter to Bentley, in denying that one material
body can act at a distance on another material body, Newton also denies
that gravity is "innate" or "inherent" in matter, or that it is part of the
"essence" of matter. He apparently thinks that to conceive of gravity as
"innate" or "inherent" in matter is to think of it as due to no other physical process, entity, or medium between material bodies. Hence the claim
about innateness or inherence amounts to the claim that there is action
at a distance. Since Newton takes the latter to be simply unintelligible,
it stands to reason that he rejects the claim concerning its inherence in
matter. One way of avoiding the invocation of distant action, along with
the claim about gravity's innateness or inherence in matter, is to leave open
the possibility that gravity is due to an aetherial medium that acts on, and
even penetrates, all matter. The aether's ubiquity throughout space might
ensure that its action is only local in character.[22] And Newton attempts
to account for the fact that the force of gravity is inversely proportional to
the square of the distance between any two bodies by proposing that the
density of the aether varies as one's distance from a given body increases.
According to this hypothesis, the aether "impels" bodies to move toward
one another; this action appears to earth-bound observers as that of an
attractive force. The connection and import of these claims remains of
continuing scholarly interest. The postulation of the aether also raises
the question of how to understand Newton's considered attitude toward
hypotheses.

Hypotheses

One of the recurring themes in Newton's discussions of his predecessors'
and interlocutors' strategies in natural philosophy – especially those of
Descartes and Leibniz – is the question of the proper role of "hypotheses" in systematic enquiries into nature.[23] Indeed, one of Newton's most
famous pronouncements in the *Principia* is: "hypotheses non fingo," or

---

[22] Newton himself speculated about the characteristics an aether might have in query 21 to the *Opticks*;
he did not think there was sufficient independent empirical evidence indicating the existence of
an aether to place his speculation within the main text of the *Opticks*.

[23] For a discussion of the development in Newton's conception of hypotheses over time, see I.
Bernard Cohen, "Hypotheses in Newton's Philosophy," *Physis: Rivista Internazionale di Storia
della Scienza* 8 (1966): 163–84.

"I feign no hypotheses."[24] This phrase, which was added to the second edition of the text, is often taken to mean that Newton eschews all hypothetical reasoning in natural philosophy. In fact, Newton does not systematically avoid hypotheses; rather, he believes that within the boundaries of experimental philosophy – the *Principia* and the *Opticks* (excepting the queries) can be considered works in this area – one may not hypothesize, but it is not improper to propose hypotheses to prod future experimental research. Such hypothetical speculations are either reserved for the queries to the *Opticks*, or are more or less explicitly labeled as such in the optics papers from the 1670s and in the *Principia*. For instance, in the Scholium to Proposition 96 of Book I of the *Principia*, Newton discusses hypotheses concerning light rays. Similarly, in query 21 of the *Opticks*, he proposes that there might be an aether whose differential density accounts for the gravitational force acting between bodies, as we have just seen.

Why, then, is a given proposition characterized as a hypothesis? The case of the postulated aether in query 21 indicates an answer, for the most salient fact about the aether is that Newton lacks independent experimental evidence indicating its existence. This coheres with Cotes's rejection, in his preface to the *Principia's* second edition, of the common hypothesis that planetary motion can be explained via vortices on the grounds that their existence does not enjoy independent empirical confirmation [this volume, p. 52]. So hypotheses make essential reference to entities whose existence lacks independent empirical support. With such support, one's explanation would successfully shake off the mantle of "hypothesis." Newton's contention, then, is that both Descartes and Leibniz proceed in a "hypothetical" manner by attempting to explain phenomena through invoking the existence of entities for which there is no independent empirical evidence.[25]

Newton's attitude toward hypotheses is connected in another way to his skepticism concerning Cartesian and Leibnizian natural philosophy. In the General Scholium, he contends: "For whatever is not deduced from

---

[24] We owe this translation of the phrase to Alexandre Koyré, who first noted that Newton uses the word "feign" in a parallel discussion in English: *From the Closed World to the Infinite Universe* (Baltimore, MD: Johns Hopkins University Press, 1957), 229 and 299 n. 12.

[25] In order to account for the motions of the planetary bodies in his *Tentamen*, for instance, Leibniz introduces *ex hypothesi* the premise that some kind of fluid surrounds, and is contiguous to, the various planetary bodies, and then argues that this fluid must be in motion. See the *Tentamen* in Gottfried Wilhelm Leibniz, *Mathematische Schriften*, ed. C. Gerhardt (Berlin, 1849), vol. 6: 149, and Domenico Bertoloni Meli, *Equivalence and Priority: Newton vs. Leibniz* (Oxford: Oxford University Press, 1993), 128–9.

the phenomena must be called a hypothesis; and hypotheses, whether metaphysical or physical, or based on occult qualities, or mechanical, have no place in experimental philosophy" (p. 92 in this volume). It therefore appears that hypotheses may be generated from various sorts of metaphysical principle or view, and so the exclusion of hypotheses may also represent a way of distinguishing "experimental philosophy" from metaphysics. Indeed, one of Newton's primary complaints against both the Cartesians and Leibniz is that they mix metaphysical with experimental concerns, that they infuse metaphysical views, which he thinks are always questionable and highly disputable, into their experimental philosophy, thereby preventing the latter from proceeding on a secure empirical footing. His discussion of hypotheses is one of several ways in which Newton raises this concern about his predecessors' methods.

But how does this interpretation of Newton's attitude toward hypotheses illuminate his conception of the cause of gravity? After all, in the General Scholium, "hypotheses non fingo" concerns the postulation of a cause for gravity. It is sometimes claimed that Newton took any "physical" characterization of gravity – any characterization of its cause – to involve hypotheses, the very type of assumption he strove so stridently to expunge from physics. However, Newton does not rule out causal explanations of gravity because they necessarily involve hypotheses. Rather, when Newton wrote the General Scholium there was no independent empirical evidence to support the relevant causal explanations of gravity, so they remained merely hypothetical. Hence "hypotheses non fingo" means that we have insufficient data to characterize gravity physically; it means neither that we have grounds for ending the search for such data, nor that attempts to use new data to produce a physical characterization would involve a sullying of physics by hypotheses. The "physical" treatment of force Newton eschews in the *Principia* must await sufficient empirical findings.

The queries to the *Opticks*

There are many salient differences between Newton's two great works, the *Principia* and the *Opticks*, despite the tremendous influence each had on subsequent research in their respective scientific fields in the eighteenth century and beyond. As I. Bernard Cohen has astutely shown, Newton's choice of the vernacular rather than Latin for the presentation of his optical views may reflect his opinion that English was more appropriate for a field like optics, which had not yet achieved the same status as the science of the *Principia*, in part because it had not yet been sufficiently mathematized.[26] Although Newton did include certain important – and influential – speculative remarks in the *Principia*, most notably in the famous General Scholium, the *Opticks* ends, in its later editions, with a series of thirty-one "queries" in which Newton presents speculations on an extremely wide range of natural phenomena, including some in what we would now call biology, chemistry, and physics. These queries indicate Newton's avowed willingness to consider all manner of hypotheses: he argues in the "Account," which I discuss below, that he explicitly separates these questions from the rest of the text of the *Opticks* and labels them as such to avoid the charge that he has "feigned" the hypotheses.

This highlights again the subtlety of Newton's attitude toward hypotheses, which is easily missed. As we have seen, some proposition – for instance, "The motion of the planets in elliptical orbits around the sun is caused by the action of an aether with differential density at distinct points in space" – will be labeled a hypothesis if there is no, or at any rate obviously insufficient, independent empirical evidence indicating the existence of the postulated entity, in this case the aether. But that same proposition can be considered as a prod to further empirical research; it is not "feigned" unless one adopts an unwarranted epistemic attitude toward it, for instance, if one asserts it to be the correct explanation of some documented natural phenomenon. The queries, then, press us to distinguish the epistemic status of a proposition vis-à-vis a relevant body of empirical data, and the proper epistemic attitude toward such a proposition, given all the relevant empirical data. Newton does not feign hypotheses in the General Scholium to the *Principia* in order to present a causal explanation of gravity – for instance, he does not contend that gravity must be due to the operation of an aether – but he is certainly

---

[26] Just as intriguingly, Cohen has emphasized that Newton left his name off the title page of the *Opticks*, perhaps another indication of the less than fully systematic and scientific character of the work in that field. See I. Bernard Cohen, "The Case of the Missing Author: The Title Page of Newton's *Opticks* (1704), with Notes on the Title Page of Huygens's *Traité de la Lumière*," in Buchwald and Cohen (eds.), *Isaac Newton's Natural Philosophy*.

willing to speculate about the possible properties of an aether in query 21 to the *Opticks*, as he had already done at the end of his 1679 letter to Boyle. Beginning already with his work in optics in the early 1670s, Newton consistently felt that his interlocutors were insufficiently careful regarding such epistemic matters, a fact nicely highlighted by Newton's own speculations in the queries.

Newton's relation to Leibniz

The most influential philosophical correspondence of the eighteenth century, that between Leibniz and Newton's stalwart defender, the theologian Samuel Clarke, was preceded by a little-known, reasonably brief, but also quite significant exchange in 1693 between Leibniz and Newton himself (they had previously corresponded nearly twenty years earlier on other matters). After praising Newton for his tremendous accomplishment in the *Principia*, Leibniz contends that Newton's theory of gravity fails to indicate not only the cause of gravity, as was acknowledged explicitly by Newton himself, but also the cause of the phenomena treated by Newton's theory, especially the planetary orbits. As indicated by Leibniz's own account of celestial phenomena, the *Essay on the Causes of Celestial Motions* (or *Tentamen*) of 1689, he thought that the phenomena in question must be understood as following from some cause that meets what he took to be the strictures of the mechanical philosophy: they must follow from bits of matter in motion that transfer motion only through impact on other bits of matter. Newton had famously failed to uncover any such cause, or mechanism.

Newton's own response to this well-known charge, one unfortunately not taken up by Clarke in his later correspondence with Leibniz, was that although he had indeed failed to uncover the cause of gravity, he nonetheless had established that gravity itself is causal. That is, from Newton's point of view, gravity had been successfully identified as the cause of the celestial phenomena in question, particularly the planetary orbits. This claim is crucial because it brings us to the heart of Newton's understanding of gravity in particular, and of force in general, especially as it is articulated in the sections of the *Principia* reproduced in this volume. As the Definitions make explicit, Newton thinks of gravity as one type of centripetal force, and the latter is defined at the outset as a cause of changes in states of motion.[27] Hence it should come as no surprise to find Newton warning Leibniz against inferring that gravity itself is not a cause from the fact that Newton had failed to uncover gravity's cause. For Newton had defined gravity from the outset as one type of cause, as one sort of force that alters the states of motion of material bodies. Precisely how Newton can conceive of gravity itself as a cause without invoking action at a distance, if that is possible at all, is a topic of continuing interest.

Newton's correspondence with Leibniz in 1693, albeit brief, is of considerable significance because it highlights Newton's attempt to convince Leibniz that the theory of gravity in the *Principia* is sufficient to undermine the vortex theory favored by Leibniz. It is also significant because it represents an interaction between them that was not tainted by the controversy over the calculus; the latter did not seriously flare up until the English Newtonian John Keill claimed in 1708 that Leibniz had stolen the calculus from Newton. This controversy, with all its nationalist undertones and hyperbolic rhetoric, would taint much of the more famous correspondence between Leibniz and Clarke, and would eventually see Newton write and publish a supposedly anonymous response to a supposedly impartial review of the calculus affair by a committee convened under the auspices of the Royal Society (the "Account").

Nearly twenty years after their illuminating exchange in 1693, Leibniz and Newton narrowly missed a second opportunity to discuss their philosophical differences. In May of 1712, Leibniz wrote a letter to Nicholas Hartsoeker that was highly critical of the Newtonians; it was later published in the *Memoirs of Literature*, a journal to which Roger Cotes, the editor of the *Principia*'s second edition, held a subscription. After Cotes brought Leibniz's criticisms to Newton's attention – especially the claim that the *Principia* renders gravitation a "perpetual miracle" because it does not specify the physical mechanism underlying it – Newton wrote an intriguing, but only posthumously published, rebuttal. Here is part of Newton's paraphrase of Leibniz's original letter: "But he [i.e. Leibniz] goes on and tells us that God could not create planets that should

---

[27] See pp. 60–1 in this volume. It is widely believed that Newton named the type of force that "tends to a centre as to a point" *centripetal* in honor of Huygens, who dubbed the force with the opposite tendency *centrifugal*.

move round of themselves without any cause that should prevent their removing through the tangent. For a miracle at least must keep the planet in" (see this volume p. 117). Newton's response to this Leibnizian charge, I believe, is illuminating: "But certainly God could create planets that should move round of themselves without any other cause than gravity that should prevent their removing through the tangent. For gravity without a miracle may keep the planets in" (ibid.). The crux of the retort, then, is that gravity causes the planets to follow their orbital paths rather than their inertial trajectories along the tangents to those orbits. Newton apparently held this conception of gravity throughout much of his life.

By the time Newton wrote his "Account" of the Royal Society report concerning the calculus affair, the controversy between Newton and Leibniz had effected a significant rift between their followers in England and on the Continent. Not surprisingly, therefore, Newton's "Account" is highly polemical and includes many incendiary remarks, but it also includes several intriguing comparisons between what he takes to be the Newtonian "experimental philosophy" and the "metaphysics" promoted by Leibniz; we reproduce those remarks in this volume. The text indicates, among other things, that Newton was acquainted not just with Leibniz's contributions to mathematics and dynamics, but with at least some of his more narrowly metaphysical work, including his view of the pre-established harmony. It reworks familiar themes from the 1693 correspondence with Leibniz, and from Leibniz's exchange with Clarke, such as their differing attitudes toward the so-called mechanical philosophy, but it also highlights Newton's own conception of the important philosophical elements of the *Principia* and of the *Opticks* through extensive quotation from those texts. Each of the passages Newton singles out as salient is reprinted in this volume.

One should not overemphasize Newton's philosophical interests or achievements: to the extent that they are distinct from his results in mathematics, mechanics, and optics, they certainly pale in comparison to the latter. One should also not overlook Newton's skepticism concerning the practice of philosophy in his day, a time when the influence of late scholasticism was still felt, and when a prodigious quantity of speculation accompanied the rise of what we call modern philosophy and modern science. Newton was keenly aware of the limits of the knowledge of nature

achieved in this period, limits that he thought of his interlocutors and crit-
ics as trespassing by proposing hypotheses. As he wrote to Robert Boyle
in 1679, in "natural philosophy" there is "no end of fancying." Happily
for us, this did not prevent Newton from contributing substantially to the
development of early modern philosophy.

Chronology

1689	Leibniz's *Tentamen* appears in *Acta Eruditorum*
1690	Newton corresponds with Locke; publication of Locke's *Essay Concerning Human Understanding* in London
1691/2	Death of Boyle; Boyle's will endows the Royal Society's Boyle Lectures in defense of religion
1692/3	Richard Bentley and Newton correspond extensively; Bentley delivers the first Boyle Lectures in London
1693	Leibniz and Newton correspond
1696	Newton appointed Warden of the Mint in London
1703	Newton elected President of the Royal Society (a position he retained until his death in 1727)
1704	First edition of the *Opticks* is published in London (with sixteen queries) by the printers to the Royal Society
1704/5	Samuel Clarke delivers the Boyle Lectures in London
1705	Newton is knighted by Queen Anne at a grand ceremony in Cambridge
1706	First edition of the Latin translation of the *Opticks*, prepared by Samuel Clarke, is published in London (with the original sixteen, plus seven new, queries)
1713	Second edition of the *Principia*, edited by Roger Cotes, is published in Cambridge
1713	The *Commercium Epistolicum*, a partisan account of the calculus controversy overseen by Newton, appears in the Royal Society's *Philosophical Transactions*
1715	Newton anonymously publishes "Account of the *Commercium Epistolicum*" in the *Philosophical Transactions*
1715–16	Clarke and Leibniz correspond extensively via Princess Caroline of Wales
1716	Death of Leibniz in November
1717	Clarke has his correspondence with Leibniz published in London
1718	Second edition of the *Opticks* is published in London (with thirty-one queries)
1721	Third edition of the *Opticks* is published in London (virtually unchanged from the second edition)
1726	Third edition of *Principia* published in London
1727	Death of Newton in March

Further reading

Classic works on Newton and his influence include Ferdinand Rosenberger's *Isaac Newton und seine physikalischen Principien* (Leipzig: J. A. Barth, 1895), Léon Bloch's *La Philosophie de Newton* (Paris: Libraires Félix Alcan, 1903), Alexandre Koyré's *Newtonian Studies* (Cambridge, MA: Harvard University Press, 1965), and I. Bernard Cohen's *The Newtonian Revolution* (Cambridge: Cambridge University Press, 1980). Influential treatments of somewhat more specialized topics include Mary Hesse, *Forces and Fields: The Concept of Action at a Distance in the History of Physics* (London: Thomas Nelson and Sons, 1961), Richard Westfall, *Force in Newton's Physics: The Science of Dynamics in the Seventeenth Century* (London: Macdonald, 1971), Ernan McMullin, *Newton on Matter and Activity* (Notre Dame, IN: University of Notre Dame Press, 1978), and A. I. Sabra, *Theories of Light from Descartes to Newton* (Cambridge: Cambridge University Press, 1981, second edition), which is philosophically astute.

Because the field of Newtonian studies is flourishing, the relevant literature is vast. For excellent selections of papers and articles on diverse topics, see the classic collection *The Annus Mirabilis of Sir Isaac Newton 1666–1966*, edited by Robert Palter (Cambridge, MA: MIT Press, 1970), and the more recent collections, *Philosophical Perspectives on Newtonian Science*, edited by Philip Bricker and R. I. G. Hughes (Cambridge, MA: MIT Press, 1990), *Isaac Newton's Natural Philosophy*, edited by Jed Buchwald and I. Bernard Cohen (Cambridge, MA: MIT Press, 2001), and *The Cambridge Companion to Newton*, edited by I. Bernard Cohen and George Smith (Cambridge: Cambridge University Press, 2002); the last work contains an extensive bibliography of works by and about Newton.

Important studies of the *Principia* and its background include John Herivel, *The Background to Newton's "Principia": A Study of Newton's Dynamical Researches in the Years 1664–1684* (Oxford: Clarendon Press, 1965), I. Bernard Cohen, *Introduction to Newton's "Principia"* (Cambridge, MA: Harvard University Press, 1971), Bruce Brakenridge, *The Key to Newton's Dynamics: The Kepler Problem and the "Principia,"* with translations by Mary Ann Rossi (Berkeley: University of California Press, 1995), Dana Densmore, *Newton's "Principia": The Central Argument*, with translations and illustrations by William Donahue (Santa Fe, NM: Green Lion Press, 1995), François DeGandt, *Force and Geometry in Newton's "Principia"*, translated by Curtis Wilson (Princeton: Princeton University Press, 1995), S. Chandrasekhar, *Newton's "Principia" for the Common Reader* (Oxford: Oxford University Press, 1995), and Nicholas Guicciardini, *Reading the "Principia": The Debate on Newton's Mathematical Methods for Natural Philosophy from 1687 to 1736* (Cambridge: Cambridge University Press, 1999). On Newton's optics, see Sabra's *Theories of Light from Descartes to Newton*, A. R. Hall's *And All Was Light: An Introduction to Newton's "Opticks"* (Oxford: Clarendon Press, 1993), and Alan Shapiro's *Fits, Passions, and Paroxysms: Physics, Method, and Chemistry and Newton's Theories of Colored Bodies and Fits of Easy Reflection* (Cambridge: Cambridge University Press, 1993).

The standard biography of Newton remains Richard Westfall's magisterial *Never at Rest* (Cambridge: Cambridge University Press, 1980), which is available in a condensed version as *The Life of Isaac Newton* (Cambridge: Cambridge University Press, 1993). For early biographical views of Newton, see *Isaac Newton, Eighteenth-Century Perspectives*, edited by A. Rupert Hall (Oxford: Oxford University Press, 1999). For a shorter discussion, see I. Bernard Cohen's entry on Newton in the *Dictionary of Scientific Biography*, volume 10 (New York: Scribner's, 1974). The best account of Newton's intellectual disputes with Leibniz is Domenico Bertoloni Meli's *Equivalence and Priority: Newton vs. Leibniz* (Oxford: Oxford University Press, 1993). The broader cultural and historical context of Newton's work is explored in Betty Jo Teeter Dobbs and Margaret Jacobs, *Newton and the Culture of Newtonianism* (Atlantic Highlands, NJ: Humanities Press, 1995).

The principal sources for the scholarly study of Newton's oeuvre include: *Isaac Newton's "Philosophiae Naturalis Principia Mathematica," the Third Edition with Variant Readings*, edited by Alexandre Koyré and I.

Bernard Cohen, with Anne Whitman (Cambridge, MA: Harvard University Press, 1972), along with the new standard translation, *The "Principia": Mathematical Principles of Natural Philosophy, a New Translation*, translated by I. Bernard Cohen and Anne Whitman, with Julia Budenz (Berkeley: University of California Press, 1999), and *Opticks: or, A Treatise of the Reflections, Refractions, Inflections and Colours of Light* (New York: Dover, 1952), which is based on the fourth edition of 1730. Some of the more important articles and papers written by Newton are available in these collections: *Isaac Newton's Theological Manuscripts*, edited by Herbert McLachlan (Liverpool: Liverpool University Press, 1950), *Isaac Newton's Papers and Letters on Natural Philosophy*, edited by I. Bernard Cohen and Robert Schofield (Cambridge, MA: Harvard University Press, 1978, revised edition), *Unpublished Scientific Papers of Isaac Newton*, edited by A. R. Hall and Marie Boas Hall (Cambridge: Cambridge University Press, 1962), *The Mathematical Papers of Isaac Newton*, edited by D. T. Whiteside (Cambridge: Cambridge University Press, 1967–81), and *The Optical Papers of Isaac Newton*, volume 1: *The Optical Lectures of 1670–1672*, edited by Alan Shapiro (Cambridge: Cambridge University Press, 1984). Newton's undergraduate notebooks from Trinity College are available as *Certain Philosophical Questions: Newton's Trinity Notebook*, edited by J. E. McGuire and Martin Tamny (Cambridge: Cambridge University Press, 1983). For a complete reproduction of Newton's letters, see *The Correspondence of Isaac Newton*, edited by Herbert Turnbull, John Scott, A. R. Hall, and Laura Tilling (Cambridge: Cambridge University Press, 1959–77). The Newton Project at Imperial College, London is an ongoing program to make all of Newton's works, including extensive unpublished manuscript materials, available to the public via the Internet: <http://www.newtonproject.ic.ac.uk>.

Note on texts and translations

I Correspondence with Robert Boyle [1679]. Newton's letter to Boyle of 28 February 1678/9 is taken from the version in *Correspondence of Isaac Newton*, edited by H. W. Turnbull et al. (Cambridge: Cambridge University Press, 1959–), volume 2: 288–96.

II De Gravitatione [date unknown; likely before 1685]. With my assistance, Christian Johnson (University of Notre Dame) revised and corrected the translation of *De Gravitatione* in *Unpublished Scientific Writings of Isaac Newton*, edited by A. R. Hall and Marie Boas Hall (Cambridge: Cambridge University Press, 1962), which also includes a transcription of the original Latin text. Johnson and I have attempted to follow Newton's own English usage in other texts when translating the Latin of *De Gravitatione*. We have consulted two other editions: *De La Gravitation, ou, les Fondements de la Méchanique Classique*, edited by Marie-Françoise Biarnais (Paris: Les Belles Lettres, 1985); and, *Über die Gravitation . . . Texts zu den philosophischen Grundlagen der klassischen Mechanik*, edited and translated by Gernot Böhme (Frankfurt am Main: Vittorio Klostermann, 1988); the latter includes a facsimile of the original Latin manuscript. We also consulted Howard Stein's (partial) translation of the text; we are grateful to Stein for sharing his unpublished work with us.

III Philosophiae Naturalis Principia Mathematica [1687, first edition]. The excerpts are from *The "Principia": Mathematical Principles of Natural Philosophy*, translated by I. Bernard Cohen and Anne Whitman, with the assistance of Julia Budenz (Berkeley: University of

California Press, 1999); this is based on the third edition of 1726, the last in Newton's lifetime. The excerpts are reprinted here with the kind permission of the University of California Press.

IV Correspondence with Richard Bentley [1692–3]. The four letters to Bentley, written between 10 December 1692 and 25 February 1693, are from the version in *Correspondence of Isaac Newton*, volume 3: 233–6, 238–40, 244, 253–6.

V Correspondence with G. W. Leibniz [1693/1712].

(a) Leibniz's letter to Newton on 7 March 1693 and Newton's reply on 16 October 1693 are taken from the translation in *Correspondence of Isaac Newton*, volume 3: 258–9 and 286–7, respectively.

(b) Leibniz's letter to Hartsoeker on 10 February 1711 is from the English translation in *Memoirs of Literature*, volume 3: 453–460 (London, second edition, 1722, a reprint of the first edition of 1712); this is the version Cotes and Newton read. The letter is also available in *Die Philosophischen Schriften von Gottfried Wilhelm Leibniz*, edited by C. J. Gerhardt (Leipzig: Alfred Lorenz, 1931), volume 3: 516–21.

(c) Newton's posthumously published response to (b), written to the editor of the *Memoirs of Literature* sometime after 5 May 1712, is from the version in *Correspondence of Isaac Newton*, volume 5: 298–300.

VI Correspondence with Roger Cotes [1713]. Newton's letter to Cotes of 28 March 1713, along with a draft of that letter, are taken from the versions in *Correspondence of Isaac Newton*, volume 5: 396–7 and 398–9, respectively.

VII An Account of the Book Entitled *Commercium Epistolicum* [1715]. Newton's anonymously published review of the *Commercium Epistolicum*, the Royal Society's report concerning the calculus dispute with Leibniz, is taken from the version in *Philosophical Transactions*, volume 29 (1714–16): 222–4.

VIII Opticks [1721]. The excerpts from the queries are from the last edition published in Newton's lifetime, *Opticks, or, A Treatise of the Reflections, Refractions, Inflections, and Colours of Light* (London, 1721, 3rd edn.), with the exception of the numbers provided on p. 128, which have been altered to match those of the fourth edition (London, 1730).

I

Correspondence with Robert Boyle [1679]

NEWTON TO BOYLE

Cambridge, 28 February 1678/9

Honoured Sir,

I have so long deferred to send you my thoughts about the physical qualities we spoke of, that did I not esteem myself obliged by promise, I think I should be ashamed to send them at all. The truth is, my notions about things of this kind are so indigested, that I am not well satisfied myself in them; and what I am not satisfied in, I can scarce esteem fit to be communicated to others; especially in natural philosophy, where there is no end of fancying. But because I am indebted to you, and yesterday met with a friend, Mr. Maulyverer,[1] who told me he was going to London, and intended to give you the trouble of a visit, I could not forbear to take the opportunity of conveying this to you by him.

1. It being only an explication of qualities, which you desire of me, I shall set down my apprehensions in the form of suppositions, as follows. And first, I suppose, that there is diffused through all places an aethereal substance, capable of contraction and dilatation [i.e. dilation], strongly elastic, and in a word much like air in all respects, but far more subtle.

2. I suppose this aether pervades all gross bodies, but yet so as to land rarer in their pores than in free spaces, and so much the rarer, as their pores are less. And this I suppose (with others) to be the cause, why light incident on those bodies is refracted towards the perpendicular; why two

---

[1] Newton most likely meant Thomas Mauliverer, who attended Trinity College, Cambridge as an undergraduate in the early 1660s, as did Newton.

well polished metals cohere in a receiver exhausted of air; why mercury stands sometimes up to the top of a glass pipe, though much higher than 30 inches; and one of the main causes, why the parts of all bodies cohere; also the cause of filtration, and of the rising of water in small glass pipes above the surface of the stagnating water they are dipped into: for I suspect the other may stand rarer, not only in the insensible pores of bodies, but even in the very sensible cavities of those pipes. And the same principle may cause menstruums [i.e. solvents] to pervade with violence the pores of the bodies they dissolve, that surrounding [the] aether, as well as the atmosphere, pressing them together.

3. I suppose the rarer aether within bodies, and the denser without them, not to be terminated in a mathematical superficies, but to grow gradually into one another; the external aether beginning to grow rarer, and the internal to grow denser, at some little distance from the superficies of the body, and running through all intermediate degrees of density in the intermediate spaces. And this may be the cause why light, in Grimaldo's experiment, passing by the edge of a knife, or other opaque body, is turned aside and as it were refracted, and by that refraction makes several colours.[2]

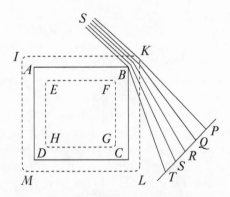

Let ABCD be a dense body, whether opaque, or transparent, E F G H the outside of the uniform aether, which is within it, I K L M the inside of the uniform aether, which is without it; and conceive the aether, which is

[2] Although it occurred years earlier, Francesco Maria Grimaldi's discovery of diffraction was published in 1665.

between E F G H and I K L M, to run through all intermediate degrees of density between that of the two uniform aethers on either side. This being supposed, the rays of the sun S B, S K, which pass by the edge of this body between B and K, ought in their passage through the unequally dense aether there, to receive a ply [bend] from the denser aether, which is on that side towards K, and that the more, by how much they pass nearer to the body, and thereby to be scattered through the space P Q R S T, as by experience they are found to be. Now the space between the limits E F G H and I K L M, I shall call the space of the aether's graduated rarity.

4. When two bodies moving towards one another come near together, I suppose the aether between them to grow rarer than before, and the spaces of its graduated rarity to extend further from the superficies of the bodies towards one another; and this, by reason, that the aether cannot move and play up and down so freely in the straight passage between the bodies, as it could before they came so near together.

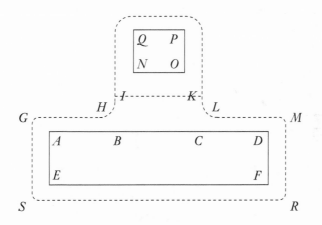

Thus, if the space of the aether's graduated rarity reach from the body ABCDFE only to the distance GHLMRS, when no other body is near it, yet may it reach farther, as to IK, when another body NOPQ approaches: and as the other body approaches more and more, I suppose the aether between them will grow rarer and rarer.

These suppositions I have so described, as if I thought the spaces of graduated aether had precise limits, as is expressed at I K L M in the first figure, and GMRS in the second: for thus I thought I could better express myself. But really I do not think they have such precise limits, but rather decay insensibly, and in so decaying, extend to a much greater distance than can easily be believed, or need be supposed.

5. Now from the fourth supposition it follows that when two bodies approaching one another come so near together as to make the aether between them begin to rarefy, they will begin to have a reluctance from being brought nearer together, and an endeavour to recede from one another: which reluctance and endeavour will increase, as they come nearer together, because thereby they cause the interjacent aether to rarefy more and more. But at length, when they come so near together that the excess of pressure of the external aether which surrounds the bodies, above that of the rarefied aether, which is between them, is so great as to overcome the reluctance which the bodies have from being brought together, then will that excess of pressure drive them with violence together, and make them adhere strongly to one another, as was said in the second supposition. For instance, in the second figure, when the bodies ED and NP are so near together that the spaces of the aether's graduated rarity begin to reach to one another and meet in the line IK; the aether between them will have suffered much rarefaction, which rarefaction requires much force, that is, much pressing of the bodies together: and the endeavour, which the aether between them has to return to its former natural state of condensation, will cause the bodies to have an endeavour of receding from one another. But on the other hand, to counterpoise this endeavour, there will not yet be any excess of density of the aether which surrounds the bodies, above that of the aether which is between them at the line I K. But if the bodies come nearer together, so as to make the aether in the mid-way-line I K grow rarer than the surrounding aether, there will arise from the excess of density of the surrounding aether a compressure of the bodies towards one another: which when by the nearer approach of the bodies it becomes so great, as to overcome the aforesaid endeavour the bodies have to recede from one another, they will then go towards one another, and adhere together. And, on the contrary, if any power [should] force them asunder to that distance, where the endeavour to recede begins to overcome the endeavour to accede, they will again leap from one another. Now hence I conceive it is chiefly that a fly walks on water without wetting her feet, and consequently without touching the water; that two polished pieces of glass are not without pressure brought to contact, no,

4

not though the one be plain, the other a little convex; that the particles of dust cannot by pressing be made to cohere, as they would do, if they did but fully touch; that the particles of tinging substances [a substance that tinges or colours][3] and salts dissolved in water do not of their own accord concrete and fall to the bottom, but diffuse themselves all over the liquor and expand still more, if you add more liquor to them. Also, that the particles of vapours, exhalations, and air, do stand at a distance from one another, and endeavour to recede as far from one another as the pressure of the incumbent atmosphere will let them: for I conceive the confused mass of vapours, air, and exhalations, which we call the atmosphere, to be nothing else but the particles of all sorts of bodies, of which the earth consists, separated from one another, and kept at a distance, by the said principle.

From these principles the actions of menstruums upon bodies may be thus explained. Suppose any tinging body, as cochineal, or logwood, be put into water;[4] so soon as the water sinks into its pores and wets on all sides any particle, which adheres to the body only by the principle in the second supposition, it takes off, or at least much diminishes the efficacy of that principle to hold the particle to the body, because it makes the aether on all sides of the particle to be of a more uniform density than before. And then the particle being shaken off, by any little motion, floats in the water, and with many such others makes a tincture [hue or colour]; which tincture will be of some lively colour, if the particles be all of the same size and density; otherwise of a dirty one. For the colours of all natural bodies whatever seem to depend on nothing but the various sizes and densities of their particles; as I think you have seen described by me more at large in another paper. If the particles be very small (as are those of salts, vitriols [sulfates of metals], and gums) they are transparent; and as they are supposed bigger and bigger, they put on these colours in order, black, white, yellow, red; violet, blue, pale green, yellow, orange, red; purple, blue, green, yellow, orange, red, etc. as is discerned by the colours, which appear at the several thicknesses of very thin plates of transparent bodies. Whence, to know the causes of the changes of colours, which are often made by the mixtures of several liquors [liquids], it is to be considered

---

[3] Boyle himself employs the terms 'menstruum' and 'tinging' (to describe a powder) in *Usefulness of the Experimental and Natural Philosophy* (London, 1663), I.i.14.

[4] Newton discusses a case where an object changes the color of water into which it is placed.

how the particles of any tincture may have their size or density altered by the infusion of another liquor.

When any metal is put into common water, the water cannot enter into its pores, to act on it and dissolve it. Not that water consists of too gross parts for this purpose, but because it is unsociable to metal. For there is a certain secret principle in nature, by which liquors are sociable to some things, and unsociable to others. Thus water will not mix with oil, but readily with spirit of wine, or with salts. It sinks also into wood, which quicksilver will not; but quicksilver sinks into metals which, as I said, water will not. So aqua fortis [nitric acid] dissolves silver and not gold, aqua regis [a mixture of nitric and hydrochloric acid] gold and not silver, etc.[5] But a liquor which is of itself unsociable to a body may, by the mixture of a convenient mediator, be made sociable. So molten lead, which alone will not mix with copper, or with regulus of Mars [a fusion of antimony sulphide with iron], by the addition of tin is made to mix with either. And water, by the mediation of saline spirits, will mix with metal. Now when any metal is put in water impregnated with such spirits, as into aqua fortis, aqua regis, spirit of vitriol [sulphuric acid], or the like, the particles of the spirits as they, in floating in the water, strike on the metal will by their sociableness enter into its pores and gather round its outside particles and, by advantage of the continual tremor the particles of the metal are in, hitch themselves in by degrees between those particles and the body, and loosen them from it; and the water entering into the pores together with the saline spirits, the particles of the metal will be thereby still more loosed, so as, by that motion the solution puts them into, to be easily shaken off, and made to float in the water: the saline particles still encompassing the metallic ones as a coat or shell does a kernel, after the manner expressed in the annexed figure. In which figure I have made the particles round, though they may be cubical, or of any other shape.

---

[5] Here Newton employs standard alchemical symbols to denote silver, gold, etc.

If into a solution of metal thus made be poured a liquor abounding with particles, to which the former saline particles are more sociable than to the particles of the metal (suppose with particles of salt of tartar [potassium carbonate]) then so soon as they strike on one another in the liquor, the saline particles will adhere to those more firmly than to the metalline ones, and by degrees be wrought off from those to enclose these. Suppose A [is] a metalline particle, enclosed with saline ones of spirit of nitre [potassium nitrate], and E a particle of salt of tartar, contiguous to two of the particles of spirit of nitre b and c, and suppose the particle E is impelled by any motion towards d, so as to roll about the particle c, till it touch the particle d, the particle b adhering more firmly to E than to A, will be forced off from A.

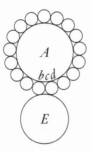

And by the same means the particle E, as it rolls about A, will tear off the rest of the saline particles from A, one after another, till it has got them all, or almost all, about itself. And when the metallic particles are thus divested of the nitrous ones which, as a mediator between them and the water, held them floating in it, the alcalizate ones crowding for the room the metallic ones took up before, will press these towards one another, and make them come more easily together: so that by the motion they continually have in the water, they shall be made to strike on one another and then, by means of the principle in the second supposition, they will cohere and grow into clusters, and fall down by their weight to the bottom, which is called precipitation.

In the solution of metals, when a particle is loosing from the body, so soon as it gets to that distance from it where the principle of receding described in the fourth and fifth suppositions begins to overcome the principle of acceding described in the second supposition, the receding of the particle will be thereby accelerated, so that the particle shall as it were with violence leap from the body, and putting the liquor into a brisk agitation, beget and promote that heat we often find to be caused in solutions of metals. And if any particle happen to leap off thus from the body, before it be surrounded with water, or to leap off with that smartness, as to get loose from the water: the water, by the principle in the fourth and fifth suppositions, will be kept off from the particle and stand round about it, like a spherically hollow arch, not being able to come to a full contact with it any more. And several of these particles afterwards gathering into a cluster, so as by the same principle to stand at a distance from one another, without any water between them, will compose a bubble. Whence I suppose it is, that in brisk solutions there usually happens an ebullition [boiling].

This is one way of transmuting gross compact substances into aerial ones. Another way is by heat. For as fast as the motion of heat can shake off the particles of water from the surface of it, those particles by the said principle will float up and down in the air, at a distance both from one another, and from the particles of air, and make that substance we call vapour. Thus I suppose it is, when the particles of a body are very small (as I suppose those of water are) so that the action of heat alone may be sufficient to shake them asunder. But if the particles be much larger, they then require the greater force of dissolving menstruums to separate them, unless by any means the particles can be first broken into smaller ones. For the most fixed [non-volatile] bodies, even gold itself, some have said will become volatile only by breaking their parts smaller. Thus may the volatility and fixedness of bodies depend on the different sizes of their parts.

And on the same difference of size may depend the more or less permanency of aerial substances in their state of rarefaction. To understand this let us suppose A B C D to be a large piece of any metal, E F G H the limit of the interior uniform aether, and K a part of the metal at the superficies AB. If this part or particle K be so little that it reaches not to the limit E F, it is plain that the aether at its centre must be less rare than if the particle were greater, for were it greater, its centre would be further from the superficies A B, that is, in a place where the aether (by supposition) is rarer.

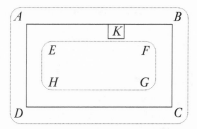

The less the particle K, therefore, the denser the aether at its centre, because its centre comes nearer to the edge A B, where the aether is denser than within the limit E F G H. And if the particle were divided from the body, and removed to a distance from it, where the aether is still denser, the aether within it must proportionally grow denser. If you consider this you may apprehend how by diminishing the particle, the rarity of the aether within it will be diminished, till between the density of the aether without, and the density of the aether within it, there be little difference, that is, till the cause be almost taken away, which should keep this and other such particles at a distance from one another. For that cause, explained in the fourth and fifth suppositions, was the excess of density of the external aether above that of the internal. This may be the reason then why the small particles of vapours easily come together and are reduced back into water unless the heat which keeps them in agitation be so great as to dissipate them as fast as they come together: but the grosser particles of exhalations raised by fermentation keep their aerial form more obstinately, because the aether within them is rarer.

Nor does the size only but the density of the particles also conduce to the permanency of aerial substances. For the excess of density of the aether without such particles above that of the aether within them is still greater. Which has made me sometimes think that the true permanent air may be of a metallic original: the particles of no substances being more dense than those of metals. This, I think, is also favoured by experience, for I remember I once read in the *Philosophical Transactions*[6] how M. Huygens at Paris found that the air made by dissolving salt of tartar would in two or three days time condense and fall down again, but the air made by

---

[6] Newton refers to "Some Experiments made in the Air-Pump by Monsieur Papin, as directed by Monsieur *Hugens*," *Philosophical Transactions* 10 (1675): 443–7. Here and elsewhere, we find a variant spelling of Christiaan Huygens's name.

dissolving a metal continued without condensing or relenting in the least. If you consider then how by the continual fermentations made in the bowels of the earth there are aerial substances raised out of all kinds of bodies, all which together make the atmosphere, and that of all these the metallic are the most permanent, you will not perhaps think it absurd that the most permanent part of the atmosphere, which is the true air, should be constituted of these: especially since they are the heaviest of all other[s], and so must subside to the lower parts of the atmosphere and float upon the surface of the earth, and buoy up the lighter exhalation and vapours to float in greatest plenty above them. Thus I say it ought to be with the metallic exhalations raised in the bowels of the earth by the action of acid menstruums, and thus it is with the true permanent air. For this as in reason it ought to be esteemed the most ponderous [heavy] part of the atmosphere because the lowest: so it betrays its ponderosity by making vapours ascend readily in it, by sustaining mists and clouds of snow, and by buoying up gross and ponderous smoke. The air also is the most gross inactive part of the atmosphere affording living things no nourishment if deprived of the more tender exhalations and spirits that float in it: and what more inactive and remote from nourishment than metallic bodies?

I shall set down one conjecture more which came into my mind now as I was writing this letter. It is about the cause of gravity. For this end I will suppose aether to consist of parts differing from one another in subtlety by indefinite degrees: that in the pores of bodies there is less of the grosser aether, in proportion to the finer, than in open spaces, and consequently that in the great body of the earth there is much less of the grosser aether, in proportion to the finer, than in the regions of the air: and that yet the grosser aether in the air affects the upper regions of the earth, and the finer aether in the earth the lower regions of the air, in such a manner that from the top of the air to the surface of the earth, and again from the surface of the earth to the centre thereof, the aether is insensibly finer and finer. Imagine now any body suspended in the air, or lying on the earth, and the aether being by the hypothesis grosser in the pores, which are in the upper parts of the body, than in those which are in its lower parts, and that grosser aether being less apt to be lodged in those pores, than the finer aether below, it will endeavour to get out and give way to the finer aether below, which cannot be without the bodies descending to make room above for it to go out into.

From this supposed gradual subtlety of the parts of aether some things above might be further illustrated, and made more intelligible, but by what has been said you will easily discern whether in these conjectures there be any degree of probability, which is all I aim at. For my own part, I have so little fancy to things of this nature that, had not your encouragement moved me to it, I should never I think have thus far set pen to paper about them. What is amiss, therefore, I hope you will the more easily pardon in

Your most humble servant and honourer,

ISAAC NEWTON

axiomatic-deductia

↓

mathematical /rational vs. *empirical*
↑
Newton

II

De Gravitatione [date unknown; probably before 1685]

A₀ It is fitting to treat the science of the weight and of the equilibrium of fluids and solids in fluids by a twofold method. To the extent that it appertains to the mathematical sciences, it is reasonable that I largely abstract it from physical considerations. And for this reason I have undertaken to demonstrate its individual propositions from abstract principles, sufficiently well known to the student, strictly and geometrically. Since this doctrine may be judged to be somewhat akin to natural philosophy, in so far as it may be applied to making clear many of the phenomena of natural philosophy and in order, moreover, that its usefulness may be particularly apparent and the certainty of its principles perhaps confirmed, I shall not be reluctant to illustrate the propositions abundantly from experiments as well, in such a way, however, that this freer method of discussion, disposed in scholia, may not be confused with the former, which is treated in lemmas, propositions and corollaries.

A₁ The foundations from which this science may be demonstrated are either definitions of certain words, or axioms and postulates no one denies. And of these I treat directly.

Definitions

The terms 'quantity', 'duration', and 'space' are too well known to be susceptible of definition by other words.[1]

---

[1] Cf. Newton's discussion in the Scholium to the *Principia* in this volume (pp. 64–70).

Definition 1. Place is a part of space which something fills completely.
Definition 2. Body is that which fills place.
Definition 3. Rest is remaining in the same place.
Definition 4. Motion is change of place.

A_2 Note. I said that a body fills place, that is, it so completely fills it that it wholly excludes other things of the same kind or other bodies, as if it were an impenetrable being. Place could be said, however, to be a part of space into which a thing enters completely; but as only bodies are here considered and not penetrable things, I have preferred to define [place] as the part of space that a thing fills.

Moreover, since body is here proposed for investigation not in so far as it is a physical substance endowed with sensible qualities, but only in so far as it is extended, mobile, and impenetrable, I have not defined it in a philosophical manner, but abstracting the sensible qualities (which philosophers also should abstract, unless I am mistaken, and assign to the mind as various ways of thinking excited by the motions of bodies),[2] I have postulated only the properties required for local motion. So that instead of physical bodies you may understand abstract figures in the same way that they are considered by geometers when they assign motion to them, as is done in Euclid's *Elements*, Book I, 4 and 8. And in the demonstration of the tenth definition, Book XI, this should be done, since it is mistakenly included among the definitions and ought rather to be demonstrated among the propositions, unless perhaps it should be taken as an axiom.[3]

Moreover, I have defined motion as change of place because motion, transition, translation, migration, and so forth seem to be synonymous words. If you prefer, let motion be transition or translation of a body from place to place.

[2] Newton refers here to the distinction between what came to be known as primary and secondary qualities, a distinction first articulated, in the modern period, by Galileo in his *Assayer* and expanded on by Boyle and Locke, among others.

[3] In Book I, proposition 4, Euclid's proof of the congruence of two triangles involves the motion of one triangle such that it achieves superposition with the other; proposition 8 similarly employs the so-called method of superposition. Definition 10 of Book XI reads as follows: "Equal and similar sold figures are those contained by similar planes equal in multitude and in magnitude" (*The Thirteen Books of Euclid's Elements*, ed. and trans. Thomas Heath [Cambridge: Cambridge University Press, 1926], vol. 3: 261). Newton takes the familiar position that this is properly understood to be a theorem rather than a definition. Some take it to be demonstrable as a theorem through the method of superposition, which may be why Newton mentions it in tandem with the above propositions from Book I.

[handwritten: Bo]

For the rest, when I suppose in these definitions that space is distinct from body, and when I determine that motion is with respect to the parts of that space, and not with respect to the position of neighboring bodies, lest this should be taken as being gratuitously contrary to the Cartesians, I shall venture to dispose of his fictions.

I can summarize his doctrine in the following three propositions:

[handwritten: 1) Each body has only one true motion]

(1) That from the truth of things only one proper motion[4] fits each body (*Principles*, Part II, articles 28, 31, 32), which may be defined as being the translation of one part of matter or of one body from the vicinity of those bodies that immediately adjoin it, and which are regarded as being at rest, to the vicinity of others (*Principles*, Part II, article 25; Part III, article 28).[5]   [handwritten: 2) Body means particle or extended whole whose parts have same velocity]

(2) That by a body – transferred in its proper motion according to this definition – may be understood not only some particle of matter, or a body composed of parts relatively at rest, but all that is transferred simultaneously, although this may, of course, consist of many parts which have different relative motions (*Principles*, Part II, article 25).

(3) That besides this motion particular to each body there can arise in it innumerable other motions through participation (or in so far as it is part of other bodies having other motions) (*Principles*, Part II, article 31), which, however, are not motions in the philosophical sense and rationally speaking (Part III, article 29) and according to the truth of things (Part II, article 25 and Part III, article 28), but only improperly and according to common sense (Part II, articles 24, 25, 28, 31; Part III, article 29). That kind of motion he seems to describe (Part II, article 24; Part III, article 28) as the action by which any body migrates from one place to another.

[handwritten: 3) Bodies are part of larger wholes + partake in the motion of these wholes]

And just as he formulates two types of motion, namely proper and derivative, so he assigns two types of place from which these motions proceed, and these are the surfaces of immediately surrounding bodies

---

4 Newton refers here, and elsewhere, to Descartes' distinction in the *Principles* between the "common" (literally, "vulgar" or "loose") and the "proper" understanding of motion (Part II, articles 34–5); cf. Newton's own distinction between "mathematical" and "common" conceptions of space, time and motion in the Scholium to the *Principia* (pp. 64–70 below).

5 In these sections of Part II of his *Principles*, Descartes defines and discusses motion, continuing on to present his laws of nature, where he articulates, among other things, an early version of the principle of inertia. In the sections of Part III cited by Newton, Descartes claims that, properly speaking, the earth does not move, given his earlier definition of motion in the *Principles*.

(Part II, article 15), and the position among any other bodies (Part II, article 13; Part III, article 29).

Indeed, not only do its absurd consequences convince us how confused and incongruous with reason this doctrine is, but Descartes seems to acknowledge the fact by contradicting himself. For he says that speaking properly and according to philosophical sense, the earth and the other planets do not move, and that he who claims they are moved because of their translation with respect to the fixed stars speaks without reason and only in the common fashion (Part III, articles 26, 27, 28, 29). Yet later he attributes to the earth and planets a tendency to recede from the sun as though from a center about which they are moved circularly, by which they are balanced at their own distances from the sun by a similar tendency of the gyrating vortex (Part III, article 140). What, then? Is this tendency to be derived from the (according to Descartes) true and philosophical rest of the planets, or rather from [their] common and non-philosophical motion? But Descartes says further that a comet has a lesser tendency to recede from the sun when it first enters the vortex, and maintaining a position among the fixed stars does not yet obey the impetus of the vortex, but with respect to it is transferred from the vicinity of the contiguous aether and so philosophically speaking gyrates round the sun, after which the matter of the vortex carries the comet along with it and so renders it at rest, according to strict philosophical sense (Part III, articles 119–20). And so the philosopher is hardly consistent who uses as the basis of philosophy the common motion which he had rejected a little before, and now rejects that motion as fit for nothing which alone was formerly said to be true and philosophical, according to the nature of things. And since the gyrating of the comet around the sun in his philosophical sense does not cause a tendency to recede from the center, which a gyration in the common sense can do, surely motion ought to be acknowledged in the common sense, rather than the philosophical.

Secondly, he seems to contradict himself when he postulates that to each body corresponds a strict motion, according to the nature of things; and yet he asserts that motion to be a product of our imagination, defining it as translation from the vicinity of bodies which are not at rest but only are seen to be at rest, even though they may instead be moving, as is more fully explained in Part II, articles 29–30. And by this he aims to avoid the difficulties concerning the mutual translation of bodies, namely, why one body is said to move rather than another, and why a boat on a flowing stream is said to be at rest when it does not change its position with respect to the banks (Part II, article 15). But so that the contradiction may be evident, imagine that someone sees the matter of the vortex to be at rest, and that the earth, philosophically speaking, is at rest at the same time; imagine also that at the same time someone else sees that the same matter of the vortex is moving in a circle, and that the earth, philosophically speaking, is not at rest. In the same way, a ship at sea will simultaneously move and not move; and that is so without taking motion in the looser common sense, according to which there are innumerable motions for each body, but in his philosophical sense, according to which, he says, there is but one in each body, and that one proper to it and corresponding to the nature of things and not to our imagination.

β₃ Thirdly, he seems hardly consistent when he posits a single motion that corresponds to each body according to the truth of things, and yet (Part II, article 31) posits innumerable motions that really are in each body. For the motions that really are in any body are in fact natural motions, and thus [are] motions in the philosophical sense and according to the truth of things, even though he would contend that they are motions in the common sense only. Add that when a whole thing moves, all the parts that constitute the whole and are translated together are really at rest, unless it is truly conceded that they move by participating in the motion of the whole, and then indeed they have innumerable motions according to the truth of things.

βᵧ But besides this, we may see from its consequences how absurd this doctrine of Descartes is. And first, just as he pointedly contends that the earth does not move because it is not transferred from the vicinity of the contiguous aether, so from these very same principles it would follow that the internal particles of hard bodies, while they are not transferred from the vicinity of immediately contiguous particles, do not have motion in the strict sense, but move only by participating in the motion of the external particles. It rather appears that the interior parts of the external particles do not move with a proper motion because they are not transferred from the vicinity of the internal parts, and I submit that only the external surface of each body moves with a proper motion and that the whole internal substance, that is the whole body, moves through participation in the motion of the external surface. The fundamental definition of motion errs, therefore, that attributes to bodies that which is suitable only to surfaces, and which denies that there can have been a more proper motion of any body at all.

B5   Secondly, if we regard only article 25 of Part II, each body has not merely a single proper motion but innumerable ones, provided that they are said to be moved properly and according to the truth of things by which the whole is properly moved. And that is because by the body whose motion he defines, he understands all that which is transferred simultaneously, and yet this may consist of parts having other motions among themselves: [for example] a vortex together with all the planets, or a ship along with everything in it floating on the sea, or a man walking on a ship together with the things he carries with him, or the wheel[s] of a clock together with its constituent metallic particles. For unless you say that the motion of the whole aggregate is not posited as proper motion and as belonging to the parts according to the truth of things, it will have to be admitted that all these motions of the wheels of the clock, of the man, of the ship, and of the vortex, are truly and philosophically speaking in the particles of the wheels[, of the man, of the ship, and of the vortex].

B6   From both of these consequences it appears further that no one motion can be said to be true, absolute and proper in preference to others, but that all – whether with respect to contiguous bodies or remote ones – are equally philosophical; and nothing more absurd than that can be imagined. For unless it is conceded that there can be a single physical motion of any body, and that the rest of its changes of relation and position with respect to other bodies are just external designations, it follows that the earth (for example) endeavors to recede[6] from the center of the sun on account of a motion relative to the fixed stars, and endeavors the less to recede on account of a lesser motion relative to Saturn and the aetherial orbit in which it is carried, and still less relative to Jupiter and the swirling aether which occasions its orbit, and also less relative to Mars and its aetherial orbit, and much less relative to other orbits of aetherial matter which, although not bearing planets, are closer to the annual orbit of the earth; and indeed relative to its own orbit it has no endeavor, because it

---

[6] We have translated Newton's "conatus" throughout as "endeavor" for two reasons. First, when writing in English and expressing related points, Newton himself uses "endeavor"; see, for instance, the letter to Boyle (this volume, p. 4). Second, Cohen translates it in this way in his "Guide to the *Principia*" (pp. 14–15), which is prefixed to the new standard translation of that work, from which we have reprinted excerpts here – see Note on Texts and Translations above.

does not move in it. Since all these endeavors and non-endeavors cannot absolutely coincide, it is rather to be said that only the natural and the absolute motion of the earth coincide, on account of which it endeavors to recede from the sun, and because of which its translations with respect to external bodies are just external designations.

♭
7   Thirdly, it follows from the Cartesian doctrine that motion can be generated where there is no force acting. For example, if God should suddenly cause the spinning of our vortex to stop, without applying any force to the earth which could stop it at the same time, Descartes would say that the earth is moving in a philosophical sense – on account of its translation from the vicinity of the contiguous fluid – whereas before he said it was at rest, in the same philosophical sense.

♭
8   Fourthly, it also follows from the same doctrine that God himself could not generate motion in some bodies even though he impelled them with the greatest force. For example, if God impelled the starry heaven together with all the most remote part of creation with any very great force so as to cause it to revolve around the earth (suppose with a diurnal motion): yet by this, according to Descartes, the earth alone and not the sky would be truly said to move (Part III, article 38), as if it would be the same whether, with a tremendous force, he would cause the skies to turn from east to west, or with a small force turn the earth in the opposite direction. But who will suppose that the parts of the earth endeavor to recede from its center on account only of a force impressed upon the heavens? Or is it not more agreeable to reason that when a force imparted to the heavens makes them endeavor to recede from the center of the gyration thus caused, they are for that reason the sole bodies properly and absolutely moved; and that when a force impressed upon the earth makes its parts endeavor to recede from the center of gyration thus caused, for that reason it is the sole body properly and absolutely moved, although there is the same relative motion of the bodies in both cases. And thus physical and absolute motion is to be designated by considerations other than translation, such translation being a merely external designation.

♭
9   Fifthly, it seems repugnant to reason that bodies should change their relative distances and positions without physical motion; but Descartes says that the earth and the other planets and the fixed stars are properly speaking at rest, and nevertheless they change their relative positions.

Sixthly, on the other hand, it seems no less repugnant to reason that of several bodies maintaining the same relative positions one should move physically while others are at rest. But if God should cause any planet to stand still and make it continually maintain the same position with respect to the fixed stars, would not Descartes say that although the stars are not moving, the planet now moves physically on account of a translation from the matter of the vortex?

β_{10} Seventhly, I ask by what reason any body is properly said to move when other bodies from whose vicinity it is transferred are not seen to be at rest, or rather when they cannot be seen to be at rest. For example, in what way can our own vortex be said to move circularly on account of the translation of matter near the circumference, from the vicinity of similar matter in other surrounding vortices, since the matter of surrounding vortices cannot be seen to be at rest, and this not only with respect to our vortex, but also in so far as those vortices are not at rest with respect to each other. For if the philosopher refers this translation not to the numerical corporeal particles of the vortices, but to the generic space (as he calls it) in which those vortices exist, at last we do agree, for he admits that motion ought to be referred to space in so far as it is distinguished from bodies.

β_{11} Lastly, that the absurdity of this position may be disclosed in full measure, I say that it follows furthermore that a moving body has no determinate velocity and no definite line in which it moves. And, what is worse, that the velocity of a body moving without resistance cannot be said to be uniform, nor the line said to be straight in which its motion is accomplished. On the contrary, there can be no motion since there can be none without a certain velocity and determination.

But that this may be clear, it is first of all to be shown that when a certain motion is finished it is impossible, according to Descartes, to assign a place in which the body was at the beginning of the motion; it cannot be said from where the body moved. And the reason is that according to Descartes, the place cannot be defined or assigned except with respect to the position of the surrounding bodies, and after the completion of some motion the position of the surrounding bodies no longer stays the same as it was before. For example, if the place of the planet Jupiter a year ago were sought now, by what procedure, I ask, can the Cartesian philosopher describe it? Not by means of the positions of the particles of the fluid matter, for the positions of these particles have greatly changed since a year ago. Nor can he describe it by the positions of the sun and fixed stars, for the unequal influx of subtle matter through the poles of the vortices towards the central stars (Part III, article 104), the undulation (article 114), inflation (article 111) and absorption of the vortices, and other more true causes, such as the rotation of the sun and stars around their own centers, the generation of spots, and the passage of comets through the heavens, change both the magnitude and positions of the stars so much that they may be adequate to designate the place sought only with an error of several miles; and still less can the place be accurately described and determined by their help, as geometry would require it to be described. Truly there are no bodies in the world whose relative positions remain unchanged with the passage of time, and certainly none which do not move in the Cartesian sense: that is, which are neither transported from the vicinity of contiguous bodies, nor are parts of other bodies so translated. And thus there is no basis from which we can at the present moment designate a place which was in the past, or say that such a place is any longer discoverable in nature. For since, according to Descartes, place is nothing but the surface of surrounding bodies or position among some other more distant bodies, it is impossible (according to his doctrine) that it should exist in nature any longer than those bodies maintain the same positions from which he takes the individual designation. And so, reasoning as in the question of Jupiter's position a year ago, it is clear that if one follows Cartesian doctrine, not even God himself could define the past position of any moving body accurately and geometrically now that a fresh state of things prevails since, on account of the changed positions of the bodies, the place does not exist in nature any longer.

Now since it is impossible to pick out the place in which a motion began – that is, the beginning of the space traversed – for this place no longer exists after the motion is completed, that traversed space, having no beginning, can have no length; and since velocity depends upon the length of the space passed over in a given time, it follows that the moving body can have no velocity, just as I wished to show at first. Moreover, what was said regarding the beginning of the space passed over should be understood concerning all the intermediate places; and thus, as the space has no beginning nor intermediate parts, it follows that there was no space passed over and thus no determinate motion, which was my second point. It follows indubitably that Cartesian motion is not motion, for it has no velocity, no determination, and there is no space or distance traversed by it. So it is necessary that the definition of places, and hence of local motion, be referred to some motionless being such as extension alone or

space in so far as it is seen to be truly distinct from bodies. And this the
Cartesian philosopher may the more willingly allow, if only he notices that
Descartes himself had an idea of extension as distinct from bodies, which
he wished to distinguish from corporeal extension by calling it generic
(*Principles*, Part II, articles 10, 12, 18). And also that the rotations of the
vortices, from which he deduced the force of the aether in receding from
their centers, and thus the whole of his mechanical philosophy, are tacitly
referred to generic extension.

In addition, since Descartes in Part II, articles 4 and 11, seems to have
demonstrated that body does not differ at all from extension, abstracting
hardness, color, weight, cold, heat, and the remaining qualities which
body can lack, so that at last there remains only its extension in length,
width, and depth, which therefore alone pertain to its essence. And as
this has been taken by many as proved, and is in my view the only reason
for having confidence in this opinion, and lest any doubt should remain
about the nature of motion, I shall reply to this argument by saying
what extension and body are, and how they differ from each other. For
since the distinction of substances into thinking and extended [entities],
or rather into thoughts and extensions, is the principal foundation of
Cartesian philosophy, which he contends to be known more exactly than
mathematical demonstrations: I consider it most important to overthrow
[that philosophy] as regards extension, in order to lay truer foundations
of the mechanical sciences.[7]

Perhaps now it may be expected that I should define extension as substance, or accident, or else nothing at all. But by no means, for it has
its own manner of existing which is proper to it and which fits neither
substances nor accidents. It is not substance: on the one hand, because it
is not absolute in itself, but is as it were an emanative effect of God and
an affection of every kind of being; on the other hand, because it is not
among the proper affections that denote substance, namely actions, such
as thoughts in the mind and motions in body. For although philosophers
do not define substance as an entity that can act upon things, yet everyone
tacitly understands this of substances, as follows from the fact that they
would readily allow extension to be substance in the manner of body if
only it were capable of motion and of sharing in the actions of body. And

---

[7] The distinction between thinking and extended substances is obviously crucial in Descartes'
Meditations, which Newton read. At the beginning of this paragraph, Newton may have had
the wax example from the Second Meditation in mind.

on the contrary, they would hardly allow that body is substance if it could not move, nor excite any sensation or perception in any mind whatsoever. Moreover, since we can clearly conceive extension existing without any subject, as when we may imagine spaces outside the world or places empty of any body whatsoever, and we believe [extension] to exist wherever we imagine there are no bodies, and we cannot believe that it would perish with the body if God should annihilate a body, it follows that [extension] does not exist as an accident inhering in some subject. And hence it is not an accident. And much less may it be said to be nothing, since it is something more than an accident, and approaches more nearly to the nature of substance. There is no idea of nothing, nor has nothing any properties, but we have an exceptionally clear idea of extension by abstracting the dispositions and properties of a body so that there remains only the uniform and unlimited stretching out of space in length, breadth and depth. And furthermore, many of its properties are associated with this idea; these I shall now enumerate not only to show that it is something, but also to show what it is.

1. In all directions, space can be distinguished into parts whose common boundaries we usually call surfaces; and these surfaces can be distinguished in all directions into parts whose common boundaries we usually call lines; and again these lines can be distinguished in all directions into parts which we call points. And hence surfaces do not have depth, nor lines breadth, nor points dimension, unless you say that coterminous spaces penetrate each other as far as the depth of the surface between them, namely what I have said to be the boundary of both or the common limit; and the same applies to lines and points. Furthermore, spaces are everywhere contiguous to spaces, and extension is everywhere placed next to extension, and so there are everywhere common boundaries of contiguous parts; that is, there are everywhere surfaces acting as boundaries to solids on this side and that; and everywhere lines in which parts of the surfaces touch each other; and everywhere points in which the continuous parts of lines are joined together. And hence there are everywhere all kinds of figures, everywhere spheres, cubes, triangles, straight lines, everywhere circular, elliptical, parabolical, and all other kinds of figures, and those of all shapes and sizes, even though they are not disclosed to sight. For the delineation of any material figure is not a new production of that figure with respect to space, but only a corporeal representation of it, so that what was formerly insensible in space now appears before

22

the senses. For thus we believe all those spaces to be spherical through which any sphere ever passes, being progressively moved from moment to moment, even though a sensible trace of that sphere no longer remains there. We firmly believe that the space was spherical before the sphere occupied it, so that it could contain the sphere; and hence as there are everywhere spaces that can adequately contain any material sphere, it is clear that space is everywhere spherical. And so of other figures. In the same way we see no material shapes in clear water, yet there are many in it which merely introducing some color into its parts will cause to appear in many ways. However, if the color were introduced, it would not constitute material shapes, but only cause them to be visible.

2. Space is extended infinitely in all directions. For we cannot imagine any limit anywhere without at the same time imagining that there is space beyond it. And hence all straight lines, paraboloids, hyperboloids, and all cones and cylinders and other figures of the same kind continue to infinity and are bounded nowhere, even though they are crossed here and there by lines and surfaces of all kinds extending transversely, and with them form segments of figures in all directions. So that you may indeed have an instance of infinity, imagine any triangle whose base and one side are at rest and the other side turns about the contiguous end of its base in the plane of the triangle so that the triangle is by degrees opened at the vertex, and meanwhile take a mental note of the point where the two sides meet, if they are produced that far: it is obvious that all these points are found on the straight line along which the fixed side lies, and that they become perpetually more distant as the moving side turns further until the two sides become parallel and can no longer meet anywhere. Now, I ask, what was the distance of the last point where the sides met? It was certainly greater than any assignable distance, or rather none of the points was the last, and so the straight line in which all those meeting points lie is in fact greater than finite. Nor can anyone say that this is infinite only in imagination, and not in fact; for if a triangle is actually drawn, its sides are always, in fact, directed towards some common point, where both would meet if produced, and therefore there is always such an actual point where the produced sides would meet, although it may be imagined to fall outside the limits of the physical universe. And so the line traced by all these points will be real, though it extends beyond all distance.

If anyone now objects that we cannot imagine extension to be infinite, I agree. But at the same time I contend that we can understand it. We can imagine a greater extension, and then a greater one, but we understand that there exists a greater extension than any we can imagine. And here, incidentally, the faculty of understanding is clearly distinguished from imagination.

Should one say further that we do not understand what an infinite being is, save by negating the limitations of a finite being, and that this is a negative and faulty conception, I deny this. For the limit or boundary is the restriction or negation of greater reality or existence in the limited being, and the less we conceive any being to be constrained by limits, the more we observe something to be attributed to it, that is, the more positively we conceive it. And thus by negating all limits the conception becomes maximally positive. 'End' [*finis*] is a word negative with respect to perception, and thus 'infinity,' since it is the negation of a negation (that is, of ends), will be a word maximally positive with respect to our perception and understanding, though it seems grammatically negative. Add [also] that positive and finite quantities of many surfaces infinite in length are accurately known to geometers. And so I can positively and accurately determine the solid quantities of many solids infinite in length and breadth and compare them to given finite solids. But this is irrelevant here.

If Descartes should now say that extension is not infinite but rather indefinite, he should be corrected by the grammarians. For the word 'indefinite' ought never to be applied to that which actually is, but always looks to a future possibility, signifying only something which is not yet determined and definite. Thus before God had decreed anything about the creation of the world (if ever he was not decreeing), the quantity of matter, the number of the stars, and all other things were indefinite; once the world was created, they were defined. Thus matter is indefinitely divisible, but is always divided either finitely or infinitely (Part I, article 26; Part II, article 34). Thus an indefinite line is one whose future length is still undetermined. And so an indefinite space is one whose future magnitude is not yet determined; for indeed that which actually is, is not to be defined, but either does or does not have boundaries and so is either finite or infinite. Nor may Descartes object that he takes space to be indefinite in relation to us; that is, we just do not know its limits and do not know positively that there are none (Part I, article 27). This is because although we are ignorant beings, God at least understands that there are no limits, not merely indefinitely but certainly and positively, and because although we negatively imagine it to transcend all limits, yet we positively and most certainly understand that it does so. But I see what Descartes feared, namely that if he should consider space infinite, it would perhaps become God because of the perfection of infinity. But by no means, for infinity is not perfection except when it is attributed to perfect things. Infinity of intellect, power, happiness, and so forth is the height of perfection; but infinity of ignorance, impotence, wretchedness, and so on is the height of imperfection; and infinity of extension is so far perfect as that which is extended.

3. The parts of space are motionless. If they moved, it would have to be said either that the motion of each part is a translation from the vicinity of other contiguous parts, as Descartes defined the motion of bodies, and it has been sufficiently demonstrated that this is absurd; or that it is a translation out of space into space, that is out of itself, unless perhaps it is said that two spaces everywhere coincide, a moving one and a motionless one. Moreover, the immobility of space will be best exemplified by duration. For just as the parts of duration are individuated by their order, so that (for example) if yesterday could change places with today and become the later of the two, it would lose its individuality and would no longer be yesterday, but today; so the parts of space are individuated by their positions, so that if any two could change their positions, they would change their individuality at the same time and each would be converted numerically into the other. The parts of duration and space are understood to be the same as they really are only because of their mutual order and position; nor do they have any principle of individuation apart from that order and position, which consequently cannot be altered.

4. Space is an affection of a being just as a being. No being exists or can exist which is not related to space in some way. God is everywhere, created minds are somewhere, and body is in the space that it occupies; and whatever is neither everywhere nor anywhere does not exist. And hence it follows that space is an emanative effect of the first existing being, for if any being whatsoever is posited, space is posited. And the same may be asserted of duration: for certainly both are affections or attributes of a being according to which the quantity of any thing's existence is individuated to the degree that the size of its presence and persistence is specified. So the quantity of the existence of God is eternal in relation to duration, and infinite in relation to the space in which he is present;

and the quantity of the existence of a created thing is as great in relation to duration as the duration since the beginning of its existence, and in relation to the size of its presence, it is as great as the space in which it is present.

Moreover, lest anyone should for this reason imagine God to be like a body, extended and made of divisible parts, it should be known that spaces themselves are not actually divisible, and furthermore, that any being has a manner proper to itself of being present in spaces. For thus the relation of duration to space is very different from that of body to space. For we do not ascribe various durations to the different parts of space, but say that all endure simultaneously. The moment of duration is the same at Rome and at London, on the earth and on the stars, and throughout all the heavens. And just as we understand any moment of duration to be diffused throughout all spaces, according to its kind, without any concept of its parts, so it is no more contradictory that mind also, according to its kind, can be diffused through space without any concept of its parts.

5. The positions, distances, and local motions of bodies are to be referred to the parts of space. And this appears from the properties of space enumerated as 1 and 4 above, and will be more manifest if you conceive that there are vacuities scattered between the particles, or if you pay heed to what I have formerly said about motion. To this it may be further added that in space there is no force of any kind that might impede, assist, or in any way change the motions of bodies. And hence projectiles describe straight lines with a uniform motion unless they meet with an impediment from some other source. But more of this later.

6. Lastly, space is eternal in duration and immutable in nature because it is the emanative effect of an eternal and immutable being. If ever space had not existed, God at that time would have been nowhere; and hence he either created space later (where he was not present himself), or else, which is no less repugnant to reason, he created his own ubiquity. Next, although we can possibly imagine that there is nothing in space, yet we cannot think that space does not exist, just as we cannot think that there is no duration, even though it would be possible to suppose that nothing whatever endures. This is manifest from the spaces beyond the world, which we must suppose to exist (since we imagine the world to be finite), although they are neither revealed to us by God, nor known through perception, nor does their existence depend upon that of the spaces within the world. But it is usually believed that these spaces are nothing; yet

indeed they are spaces. Although space may be empty of body, nevertheless it is not in itself a void; and something is there, because spaces are there, although nothing more than that. Yet in truth it must be acknowledged that space is no more space where the world exists, than where there is no world, unless perchance you would say that when God created the world in this space he at the same time created space in itself, or that if God should afterwards annihilate the world in this space, he would also annihilate the space in it. Whatever has more reality in one space than in another space belongs to body rather than to space; the same thing will appear more clearly if we lay aside that puerile and jejune prejudice according to which extension is inherent in bodies like an accident in a subject without which it cannot actually exist.

Now that extension has been described, it remains to give an explanation of the nature of body. Of this, however, the explanation must be more uncertain, for it does not exist necessarily but by divine will, because it is hardly given to us to know the limits of the divine power, that is to say, whether matter could be created in one way only, or whether there are several ways by which different beings similar to bodies could be produced. And although it scarcely seems credible that God could create beings similar to bodies which display all their actions and exhibit all their phenomena, and yet would not be bodies in essential and metaphysical constitution, as I have no clear and distinct perception[8] of this matter I should not dare to affirm the contrary, and hence I am reluctant to say positively what the nature of bodies is, but I would rather describe a certain kind of being similar in every way to bodies, and whose creation we cannot deny to be within the power of God, so that we can hardly say that it is not body.

Since each man is conscious that he can move his body at will, and believes further that other men enjoy the same power of similarly moving their bodies by thought alone, the free power of moving bodies at will can by no means be denied to God, whose faculty of thought is infinitely greater and more swift. And for the same reason it must be agreed that God, by the sole action of thinking and willing, can prevent a body from penetrating any space defined by certain limits.

If he should exercise this power, and cause some space projecting above the earth, like a mountain or any other body, to be impervious to bodies and

---

[8] Here Newton has adopted Cartesian terminology familiar to his readers.

thus stop or reflect light and all impinging things, it seems impossible that we should not consider this space really to be a body from the evidence of our senses (which constitute our sole judges in this matter); for it ought to be regarded as tangible on account of its impenetrability, and visible, opaque, and colored on account of the reflection of light, and it will resonate when struck because the adjacent air will be moved by the blow.

Thus we may suppose that there are empty spaces scattered through the world, one of which, defined by certain limits, happens by divine power to be impervious to bodies, and by hypothesis it is manifest that this would resist the motions of bodies and perhaps reflect them, and assume all the properties of a corporeal particle, except that it will be regarded as motionless. If we should suppose that that impenetrability is not always maintained in the same part of space but can be transferred here and there according to certain laws, yet so that the quantity and shape of that impenetrable space are not changed, there will be no property of body which it does not possess. It would have shape, be tangible and mobile, and be capable of reflecting and being reflected, and constitute no less a part of the structure of things than any other corpuscle, and I do not see why it would not equally operate upon our minds and in turn be operated upon, because it would be nothing other than the effect of the divine mind produced in a definite quantity of space. For it is certain that God can stimulate our perception by means of his own will, and thence apply such power to the effects of his will.

In the same way, if several spaces of this kind should be impervious to bodies and to each other, they would all sustain the vicissitudes of corpuscles and exhibit the same phenomena. And so if all of this world were constituted out of these beings, it would hardly seem to be inhabited differently. And hence these beings will either be bodies, or very similar to bodies. If they are bodies, then we can define bodies as *determined quantities of extension which omnipresent God endows with certain conditions.* These conditions are: (1) that they be mobile, and therefore I did not say that they are numerical parts of space which are absolutely immobile, but only definite quantities which may be transferred from space to space; (2) that two of this kind cannot coincide anywhere, that is, that they may be impenetrable, and hence that oppositions obstruct their mutual motions and they are reflected in accord with certain laws; (3) that they can excite various perceptions of the senses and the imagination in created minds, and conversely be moved by them, which is not surprising since the description of their origin is founded on this.

ᵭ₂ Moreover, it will help to note the following points concerning the matters already explained.

1. That for the existence of these beings it is not necessary that we suppose some unintelligible substance to exist in which as subject there may be an inherent substantial form; extension and an act of the divine will are enough. Extension takes the place of the substantial subject in which the form of the body is conserved by the divine will; and that product of the divine will is the form or formal reason of the body denoting every dimension of space in which the body is to be produced.

2. These beings will not be less real than bodies, nor (I say) are they less able to be called substances. For whatever reality we believe to be present in bodies is conferred on account of their phenomena and sensible qualities. And hence we would judge these beings, since they can receive all qualities of this kind and can similarly exhibit all these phenomena, to be no less real, if they should exist in this manner. Nor will they be any less than substances, since they will likewise subsist and acquire accidents through God alone.

3. Between extension and its impressed form there is almost the same analogy that the Aristotelians posit between prime matter and substantial forms, namely when they say that the same matter is capable of assuming all forms, and borrows the denomination of numerical body from its form.[9] For so I posit that any form may be transferred through any space, and everywhere denote the same body.

4. They differ, however, in that extension (since it [involves] "what" and "how constituted" and "how much") has more reality than prime matter, and also in that it can be understood in the same way as the form that I assigned to bodies. For if there is any difficulty in this conception it is not in the form that God imparts to space, but in the manner by which he imparts it. But that is not to be regarded as a difficulty, since the same question arises with regard to the way we move our bodies, and nevertheless we do believe that we can move them. If that were known to us, by like reasoning we should also know how God can move bodies, and

---

[9] A doctrine of so-called prime matter, according to which a type of "formless" matter would underlie various fundamental kinds of change that bodies, or elements, can undergo, is sometimes attributed to Aristotle. The attribution remains controversial: see *Physics* (190b and 193a), and *Generation and Corruption* (332a).

expel them from a certain space bounded in a given figure, and prevent the expelled bodies or any others from being able to enter it again, that is, cause that space to be impenetrable and assume the form of body.

5. Thus I have deduced a description of this corporeal nature from our faculty of moving our bodies, so that all the difficulties of the conception may at length be reduced to that; and further, so that God may appear (to our innermost consciousness) to have created the world solely by the act of will, just as we move our bodies by an act of will alone; and, moreover, so that I might show that the analogy between the divine faculties and our own may be shown to be greater than has formerly been perceived by philosophers. That we were created in God's image, holy writ testifies. And his image would shine more clearly in us if only he simulated in the faculties granted to us the power of creation in the same degree as his other attributes; nor is it an objection that we ourselves are created beings and so a share of this attribute could not have been equally granted to us. For if for this reason the power of creating minds is not delineated in any faculty of created mind, nevertheless created mind (since it is the image of God) is of a far more noble nature than body, so that perhaps it may eminently contain [body] in itself. Moreover, in moving bodies we create nothing, nor can we create anything, but we only simulate the power of creation. For we cannot make any space impervious to bodies, but we only move bodies; and at that not any we choose, but only our own bodies, to which we are united not by our own will, but by divine constitution; nor can we move bodies in any way but only in accord with those laws which God has imposed on us. If anyone, however, prefers this our power to be called the finite and lowest level of the power which makes God the creator, this no more detracts from the divine power than it detracts from his intellect that intellect belongs to us in a finite degree, particularly since we do not move our bodies by a proper and independent power but by laws imposed on us by God. Rather, if anyone should think it possible that God may produce some intellectual creature so perfect that it could, by divine accord, in turn produce creatures of a lower order, this I submit does not detract from the divine power, it posits an infinitely greater power, by which creatures would be brought forth not only directly but by other intermediate creatures. And so some may perhaps prefer to posit a soul of the world created by God, upon which he imposes the law that definite spaces are endowed with corporeal properties, rather than to believe that this function is directly discharged by God. To be sure, the world should

not be called the creature of that soul but of God alone, who creates it by constituting the soul of such a nature that the world necessarily emanates [from it]. But I do not see why God himself does not directly inform space with bodies, so long as we distinguish between the formal reason of bodies and the act of divine will. For it is contradictory that it [body] should be the act of willing or anything other than the effect which that act produces in space, which effect does not even differ less from that act than Cartesian space, or the substance of body according to the common concept; if only we suppose that they are created, that is, that they borrow existence from the will, or that they are beings of the divine reason.

Lastly, the usefulness of the idea of body that I have described is brought out by the fact that it clearly involves the principal truths of metaphysics and thoroughly confirms and explains them. For we cannot posit bodies of this kind without at the same time positing that God exists, and has created bodies in empty space out of nothing, and that they are beings distinct from created minds, but able to be united with minds. Say, if you can, which of the views, now common, elucidates any one of these truths or rather is not opposed to all of them, and leads to obscurity. If we say with Descartes that extension is body, do we not manifestly offer a path to atheism, both because extension is not created but has existed eternally, and because we have an idea of it without any relation to God, and so in some circumstances it would be possible for us to conceive of extension while supposing God not to exist? Nor is the distinction between mind and body in his philosophy intelligible, unless at the same time we say that mind has no extension at all, and so is not substantially present in any extension, that is, exists nowhere; which seems the same as if we were to say that it does not exist, or at least renders its union with body thoroughly unintelligible and impossible. Moreover, if the distinction of substances between thinking and extended is legitimate and complete, God does not eminently contain extension within himself and therefore cannot create it; but God and extension would be two separate, complete, absolute substances, and in the same sense. But on the contrary if extension is eminently contained in God, or the highest thinking being, certainly the idea of extension will be eminently contained within the idea of thinking, and hence the distinction between these ideas will not be such that both may fit the same created substance, that is, but that a body may think, and a thinking being be extended. But if we adopt the common idea (or rather lack of it) of body, according to which there resides in bodies some unintelligible reality that they call substance, in which all the qualities of the bodies are inherent, this (apart from its unintelligibility) is exposed to the same problems as the Cartesian view. Since it cannot be understood, it is impossible that its distinction from the substance of the mind should be understood. For the distinction drawn from substantial form or the attributes of substances is not enough: if bare substances do not have an essential difference, the same substantial forms or attributes can fit both, and render them by turns, if not at one and the same time, mind and body. And so if we do not understand that difference of substances deprived of attributes, we cannot knowingly assert that mind and body differ substantially. Or if they do differ, we cannot discover any basis for their union. Further, they attribute no less reality in concept (though less in words) to this corporeal substance regarded as being without qualities and forms, than they do to the substance of God, abstracted from his attributes. They conceive of both, when considered simply, in the same way; or rather they do not conceive of them, but confound them in some common apprehension of an unintelligible reality. And hence it is not surprising that atheists arise ascribing to corporeal substances that which solely belongs to the divine. Indeed, however we cast about we find almost no other reason for atheism than this notion of bodies having, as it were, a complete, absolute, and independent reality in themselves, such as almost all of us, through negligence, are accustomed to have in our minds from childhood (unless I am mistaken), so that it is only verbally that we call bodies created and dependent. And I believe that this prejudice explains why the same word, substance, is applied univocally in the schools to God and his creatures, and what philosophers, in forming the idea of body, cling to and ramble on about, when they try to form an independent idea of a thing dependent upon God. For certainly whatever cannot exist independently of God cannot be truly understood independently of the idea of God. God does not sustain his creatures any less than they sustain their accidents, so that created substance, whether you consider its degree of dependence or its degree of reality, is of an intermediate nature between God and accident. And hence the idea of it no less involves the concept of God, than the idea of accident involves the concept of created substance. And so it ought to embrace no other reality in itself than a derivative and incomplete reality. Thus the prejudice just mentioned must be laid aside, and substantial reality is to be ascribed to these kinds of attributes, which are real and intelligible things in themselves and do not need to

be inherent in a subject, rather than to the subject which we cannot
conceive as dependent, much less form any idea of it. And this we can
manage without difficulty if (besides the idea of body expounded above)
we reflect that we can conceive of space existing without any subject when
we think of a vacuum. And hence some substantial reality fits this. But
if, moreover, the mobility of the parts (as Descartes supposed) should be
involved in the idea of vacuum, everyone would freely concede that it is
corporeal substance. In the same way, if we should have an idea of that
attribute or power by which God, through the action of his will alone, can
create beings, we should readily conceive of that attribute as subsisting
by itself without any substantial subject and [thus as] involving the rest
of his attributes. But while we cannot form an idea of this attribute, nor
even of our proper power by which we move our bodies, it would be rash
to say what may be the substantial basis of mind.

D7   So much for the nature of bodies, which in explicating I judge that I
have sufficiently proved that such a creation as I have expounded is most
clearly the work of God, and that if this world were not constituted from
that creation, at least another very like it could be constituted. And since
there is no difference between the materials as regards their properties
and nature, but only in the method by which God created one and the
other, the distinction between body and extension is certainly brought
to light from this. For extension is eternal, infinite, uncreated, uniform
throughout, not in the least mobile, nor capable of inducing change of
motion in bodies or change of thought in the mind; whereas body is
opposite in every respect, at least if God did not please to create it always
and everywhere. For I should not dare to deny God that power. And if
anyone thinks otherwise, let him say where he could have created prime
matter, and whence the power of creating was granted to God. Or if there
was no beginning to that power, but he had the same eternally that he
has now, then he could have created from eternity. For it is the same to
say that there never was in God an impotence to create, or that he always
had the power to create and could have created, and that he could always
create matter. In the same way, either a space may be assigned in which
matter could not be created from the beginning, or it must be conceded
that God could have created it everywhere.

D8   Moreover, so that I may respond more concisely to Descartes' argument: let us abstract from body (as he demands) gravity, hardness, and
all sensible qualities, so that nothing remains except what pertains to its

33

essence. Will extension alone then remain? By no means. For we may also reject that faculty or power by which they [the qualities] stimulate the perceptions of thinking things. For since there is so great a distinction between the ideas of thought and of extension that it is not obvious that there is any basis of connection or relation [between them], except that which is caused by divine power, the above capacity of bodies can be rejected while preserving extension, but not while preserving their corporeal nature. Clearly the changes which can be induced in bodies by natural causes are only accidental and they do not denote that substance is really changed. But if any change is induced that transcends natural causes, it is more than accidental and radically affects the substance. And according to the sense of the demonstration, only those things are to be rejected which bodies can be deprived of, and made to lack, by the force of nature. But should anyone object that bodies not united to minds cannot directly arouse perceptions in minds, and that since there are bodies not united to minds, it follows that this power is not essential to them, it should be noticed that there is no suggestion here of an actual union, but only of a capacity of bodies by which they are capable of such a union through the forces of nature. From the fact that the parts of the brain, especially the more subtle ones to which the mind is united, are in a continual flux, new ones succeeding those which fly away, it is manifest that that capacity is in all bodies. And whether you consider divine action or corporeal nature, to remove this is no less than to remove that other faculty by which bodies are enabled to transfer mutual actions from one to another, that is, to reduce body into empty space.

However, as water offers less resistance to the motion of solid bodies passing through it than quicksilver does, and air much less than water, and aetherial spaces even less than air-filled ones, if we set aside altogether every force of resistance to the passage of bodies, we must also set aside the corporeal nature [of the medium] utterly and completely. In the same way, if the subtle matter were deprived of all forces of resistance to the motion of globules, I should no longer believe it to be subtle matter but a scattered vacuum. And so if there were any aerial or aetherial space of such a kind that it yielded without any resistance to the motions of comets or any other projectiles, I should believe that it was utterly empty. For it is impossible that a corporeal fluid should not impede the motion of bodies passing through it, assuming that (as I supposed before) it is not disposed to move at the same speed as the body (Part II, Epistle 96 to Mersenne).

However, it is manifest that every force can be removed from space only if space and body differ from one another; and hence that each can be removed is not to be denied before it has been proved that they do not differ, lest an error be let in by begging the question.

But lest any doubt remain, it should be observed from what was said earlier that there are empty spaces in nature. For if the aether were a corporeal fluid entirely without vacuous pores, however subtle its parts are made by division, it would be as dense as any other fluid, and it would yield to the motion of passing bodies with no less inertia; indeed with a much greater inertia if the projectile were porous, because then the aether would enter its internal pores, and encounter and resist not only the whole of its external surface, but also the surfaces of all the internal parts. Since the resistance of the aether is on the contrary so small when compared with the resistance of quicksilver as to be over ten or a hundred thousand times less, there is all the more reason for thinking that by far the largest part of the aetherial space is empty, scattered between the aetherial particles. The same may also be conjectured from the various gravities of these fluids, for the descent of heavy bodies and the oscillations of pendulums show that these are in proportion to their densities, or as the quantities of matter contained in equal spaces. But this is not the place to go into this.

Thus you see how fallacious and unsound this Cartesian argumentation is, for when the accidents of bodies have been rejected, there remains not extension alone, as he supposed, but also the capacities by which they can stimulate perceptions in the mind by means of various bodies. If we further reject these capacities and every power of moving, so that there only remains a precise conception of uniform space, will Descartes fabricate any vortices, any world, from this extension? Surely not, unless he first invokes God, who alone can generate new bodies in those spaces (or by restoring those capacities to the corporeal nature, as I explained above). And so in what has gone before I was correct in assigning the corporeal nature to the capacities already enumerated.

And so finally, since spaces are not the very bodies themselves, but are only the places in which bodies exist and move, I think that what I laid down concerning local motion is sufficiently confirmed. Nor do I see what more could be desired in this matter, unless perhaps I warn those for whom this is not satisfactory that by the space whose parts I have defined as places filled by bodies, they should understand the Cartesian generic space in which spaces regarded singularly, or Cartesian bodies, are moved, and so they will find hardly anything to object to in our definitions.

I have already digressed enough; let us return to the main theme.

Definition 5. Force is the causal principle of motion and rest. And it is either an external one that generates, destroys, or otherwise changes impressed motion in some body, or it is an internal principle by which existing motion or rest is conserved in a body, and by which any being endeavors to continue in its state and opposes resistance.

Definition 6. *Conatus* [endeavor] is resisted force, or force in so far as it is resisted.

Definition 7. *Impetus* is force in so far as it is impressed on a thing.

Definition 8. *Inertia* is the inner force of a body, lest its state should be easily changed by an external exciting force.

Definition 9. Pressure is the endeavor [conatus] of contiguous parts to penetrate into each other's dimensions. For if they could penetrate [each other] the pressure would cease. And pressure is only between contiguous parts, which in turn press upon others contiguous to them, until the pressure is transferred to the most remote parts of any body, whether hard, soft, or fluid. And upon this action is based the communication of motion by means of a point or surface of contact.

Definition 10. Gravity is the force in a body impelling it to descend. Here, however, by descent is not only meant a motion towards the center of the earth, but also towards any point or region, or even from any point. In this way if the endeavor [conatus] of the aether gyrating about the sun to recede from its center be taken for gravity, in receding from the sun the aether could be said to descend. And so by analogy, that plane should be called horizontal that is directly opposed to the direction of gravity or conatus. Moreover, the quantity of these powers, namely motion, force, conatus, impetus, inertia, pressure, and gravity, may be reckoned by a twofold account: that is, according to either its intension or extension.

Definition 11. The intension of any of the above mentioned powers is the degree of its quality.

Definition 12. Its extension is the quantity of space or time in which it operates.

Definition 13. Its absolute quantity is the product of its intension and its extension. So, if the quantity of the intension is 2, and the quantity of the extension 3, multiply the two together and you will have the absolute quantity 6.

Moreover, it will be helpful to illustrate these definitions via individual powers. And thus motion is either more intense or more remiss, as the space traversed in the same time is greater or less, for which reason a body is usually said to move more swiftly or more slowly. Again, motion is more or less extended as the body moved is greater or less, or as it is diffused through a larger or smaller body. And the absolute quantity of motion is composed of both the velocity and the magnitude of the moving body. So force, conatus, impetus, or inertia are more intense as they are greater in the same or an equivalent body: they are more extensive when the body is larger, and their absolute quantity arises from both. So the intension of pressure is proportional to the increase of pressure upon the surface area; its extension proportional to the surface pressed. And the absolute quantity results from the intension of the pressure and the quantity of the surface pressed. So, lastly, the intension of gravity is proportional to the specific gravity of the body; its extension is proportional to the size of the heavy body, and absolutely speaking the quantity of gravity is the product of the specific gravity and mass of the gravitating body. And whoever fails to distinguish these clearly, necessarily falls into many errors concerning the mechanical sciences.

In addition, the quantity of these powers may sometimes be reckoned according to the period of duration; for which reason there will be an absolute quantity which will be the product of intension, extension, and duration. In this way, if a body [of size] 2 is moved with a velocity 3 for a time 4, the whole motion will be $2 \times 3 \times 4$ or 24.[10]

Definition 14. Velocity is the intension of motion, slowness is remission.
Definition 15. Bodies are denser when their inertia is more intense, and rarer when it is more remiss.

The rest of the above mentioned powers have no names. It is, however, to be noted that if, with Descartes or Epicurus, we suppose rarefaction and condensation to be accomplished in the manner of relaxed or compressed

---

[10] The original manuscript erroneously has "12" in place of "24".

sponges, that is, by the dilation and contraction of pores which are either filled with, or empty of, some very subtle matter, then we ought to estimate the size of the whole body from the quantity of both its parts and its pores as in Definition 15; so that one may consider inertia to be remitted by the increase of the pores and intensified by their diminution, as though the pores, which offer no inertial resistance to change, and whose mixtures with the truly corporeal parts give rise to all the various degrees of inertia, bear some ratio to the parts.

But in order that you may conceive of this composite body as a uniform one, suppose its parts to be infinitely divided and dispersed everywhere throughout the pores, so that in the whole composite body there is not the least particle of extension without an absolutely perfect mixture of infinitely divided parts and pores. Certainly such reasoning is suitable for contemplation by mathematicians; or if you prefer the manner of the peripatetics: things seem to be captured differently in physics.

Definition 16. An elastic body is one that can be condensed by the force of pressure or compressed within the limits of a narrower space; and a nonelastic body is one that cannot be condensed by that force.

Definition 17. A hard body is one whose parts do not yield to pressure.

Definition 18. A fluid body is one whose parts yield to an overwhelming pressure. Moreover, the pressures by which the fluid is driven in any direction whatsoever (whether these are exerted merely on the external surface, or on the internal parts by the action of gravity or any other cause), are said to be balanced when the fluid rests in equilibrium. This situation obtains if the pressure is exerted in some one direction and not towards all directions at once.

Definition 19. The limits defining the surface of the body (such as wood or glass) containing the fluid, or defining the surface of the external part of the same fluid containing some internal part, constitute the vessel of fluid.

In these definitions, however, I refer only to absolutely hard or fluid bodies, for one cannot reason mathematically concerning bodies that are partially so, on account of the innumerable figures, motions, and connections of the least particles. Thus I suppose that a fluid does not consist of hard particles, but that it is of such a kind that it has no small portion or particle which is not likewise fluid. And moreover, since the physical cause of fluidity is not to be examined here, I define the parts, not as being in motion among themselves, but only as capable of motion, that is, as being everywhere so divided one from another that, although they may be supposed to be in contact and at rest with respect to one another, yet they do not cohere as though stuck together, but can be moved separately by any impressed force and can change the state of rest as easily as the state of motion if they move relatively. Indeed, I suppose that the parts of hard bodies do not merely touch each other and remain at relative rest, but that they also so strongly and firmly cohere, and are so bound together – as it were by glue – that no one of them can be moved without all the rest being drawn along with it; or rather that a hard body is not made up of conglomerate parts, but is a single undivided and uniform body which preserves its shape most resolutely, whereas a fluid body is uniformly divided at all points.

And thus I have accommodated these definitions not to physical things but to mathematical reasoning, after the manner of the geometers who do not accommodate their definitions of figures to the irregularities of physical bodies. And just as the dimensions of physical bodies are best determined by their geometry – as with the dimension of a field by plane geometry, although a field is not a true plane; and the dimension of the earth by the doctrine of the sphere, even though the earth is not pre-cisely spherical – so the properties of physical fluids and solids are best known from this mathematical doctrine, even though they are not perhaps absolutely nor uniformly fluid or solid as I have defined them here.

[Editor's note: At this point in the manuscript, Newton continues on to discuss "non-elastic fluids" for several pages, and then the text abruptly ends; the last few pages are not relevant for this volume.]

III

The *Principia* [1687, first edition]

Author's Preface to the Reader, First Edition

Since the ancients (according to Pappus) considered *mechanics* to be of the greatest importance in the investigation of nature and science and since the moderns – rejecting substantial forms and occult qualities – have undertaken to reduce the phenomena of nature to mathematical laws, it has seemed best in this treatise to concentrate on *mathematics* as it relates to natural philosophy. The ancients divided *mechanics* into two parts: the *rational*, which proceeds rigorously through demonstrations, and the *practical*. *Practical mechanics* is the subject that comprises all the manual arts, from which the subject of *mechanics* as a whole has adopted its name. But since those who practice an art do not generally work with a high degree of exactness, the whole subject of *mechanics* is distinguished from *geometry* by the attribution of exactness to *geometry* and of anything less than exactness to *mechanics*. Yet the errors do not come from the art but from those who practice the art. Anyone who works with less exactness is a more imperfect mechanic, and if anyone could work with the greatest exactness, he would be the most perfect mechanic of all. For the description of straight lines and circles, which is the foundation of *geometry*, appertains to *mechanics*. *Geometry* does not teach how to describe these straight lines and circles, but postulates such a description. For *geometry* postulates that a beginner has learned to describe lines and circles exactly before he approaches the threshold of *geometry*, and then it teaches how problems are solved by these operations. To describe straight lines and to describe circles are problems, but not problems in *geometry*. *Geometry* postulates the solution of these problems from *mechanics* and teaches the use of the problems thus solved. And *geometry* can boast that with so few principles obtained from other fields, it can do so much. Therefore *geometry* is founded on mechanical practice and is nothing other than that part of *universal mechanics* which reduces the art of measuring to exact propositions and demonstrations. But since the manual arts are applied especially to making bodies move, *geometry* is commonly used in reference to magnitude, and *mechanics* in reference to motion. In this sense *rational mechanics* will be the science, expressed in exact propositions and demonstrations, of the motions that result from any forces whatever and of the forces that are required for any motions whatever. The ancients studied this part of *mechanics* in terms of the *five powers* that relate to the manual arts [i.e. the five mechanical powers] and paid hardly any attention to gravity (since it is not a manual power) except in the moving of weights by these powers. But since we are concerned with natural philosophy rather than manual arts, and are writing about natural rather than manual powers, we concentrate on aspects of gravity, levity, elastic forces, resistance of fluids, and forces of this sort, whether attractive or impulsive. And therefore our present work sets forth mathematical principles of natural philosophy. For the basic problem of philosophy seems to be to discover the forces of nature from the phenomena of motions and then to demonstrate the other phenomena from these forces. It is to these ends that the general propositions in books 1 and 2 are directed, while in book 3 our explanation of the system of the world illustrates these propositions. For in book 3, by means of propositions demonstrated mathematically in books 1 and 2, we derive from celestial phenomena the gravitational forces by which bodies tend toward the sun and toward the individual planets. Then the motions of the planets, the comets, the moon, and the sea are deduced from these forces by propositions that are also mathematical. If only we could derive the other phenomena of nature from mechanical principles by the same kind of reasoning! For many things lead me to have a suspicion that all phenomena may depend on certain forces by which the particles of bodies, by causes not yet known, either are impelled toward one another and cohere in regular figures, or are repelled from one another and recede. Since these forces are unknown, philosophers have hitherto made trial of nature in vain. But I hope that the principles set down here will shed some light on either this mode of philosophizing or some truer one.

In the publication of this work, Edmond Halley, a man of the greatest intelligence and of universal learning, was of tremendous assistance; not only did he correct the typographical errors and see to the making of the woodcuts, but it was he who started me off on the road to this publication. For when he had obtained my demonstration of the shape of the celestial orbits, he never stopped asking me to communicate it to the Royal Society, whose subsequent encouragement and kind patronage made me begin to think about publishing it. But after I began to work on the inequalities of the motions of the moon, and then also began to explore other aspects of the laws and measures of gravity and of other forces, the curves that must be described by bodies attracted according to any given laws, the motions of several bodies with respect to one another, the motions of bodies in resisting mediums, the forces and densities and motions of mediums, the orbits of comets, and so forth, I thought that publication should be put off to another time, so that I might investigate these other things and publish all my results together. I have grouped them together in the corollaries of proposition 66 the inquiries (which are imperfect) into lunar motions, so that I might not have to deal with these things one by one in propositions and demonstrations, using a method more prolix than the subject warrants, which would have interrupted the sequence of the remaining propositions. There are a number of things that I found afterward which I preferred to insert in less suitable places rather than to change the numbering of the propositions and the cross-references. I earnestly ask that everything be read with an open mind and that the defects in a subject so difficult may be not so much reprehended as investigated, and kindly supplemented, by new endeavors of my readers.

Trinity College, Cambridge   Is. Newton
8 May 1686

Editor's Preface, Second Edition (1713)

THE LONG-AWAITED NEW EDITION of Newton's *Principles of Natural Philosophy* is presented to you, kind reader, with many corrections and additions. The main topics of this celebrated work are listed in the table of contents and the index prepared for this edition. The major additions or changes are indicated in the author's preface. Now something must be said about the method of this philosophy.

Those who have undertaken the study of natural science can be divided into roughly three classes. There have been those who have endowed the individual species of things with specific occult qualities, on which – they have then alleged – the operations of individual bodies depend in some unknown way. The whole of Scholastic doctrine derived from Aristotle and the Peripatetics is based on this. Although they affirm that individual effects arise from the specific natures of bodies, they do not tell us the causes of those natures, and therefore they tell us nothing. And since they are wholly concerned with the names of things rather than with the things themselves, they must be regarded as inventors of what might be called philosophical jargon, rather than as teachers of philosophy.

Therefore, others have hoped to gain praise for greater carefulness by rejecting this useless hodgepodge of words. And so they have held that all matter is homogeneous, and that the variety of forms that is discerned in bodies all arises from certain very simple and easily comprehensible attributes of the component particles. And indeed they are right to set up a progression from simpler things to more compounded ones, so long as they do not give those primary attributes of the particles any characteristics other than those given by nature itself. But when they take the liberty of imagining that the unknown shapes and sizes of the particles are whatever they please, and of assuming their uncertain positions and motions, and even further of feigning certain occult fluids that permeate the pores of bodies very freely, since they are endowed with an omnipotent subtlety and are acted on by occult motions: when they do this, they are drifting off into dreams, ignoring the true constitution of things, which is obviously to be sought in vain from false conjectures, when it can scarcely be found out even by the most certain observations. Those who take the foundation of their speculations from hypotheses, even if they then proceed most rigorously according to mechanical laws, are merely putting together a romance [i.e. fiction], elegant perhaps and charming, but nevertheless a romance.

There remains then the third type, namely, those whose natural philosophy is based on experiment. Although they too hold that the causes of all things are to be derived from the simplest possible principles, they assume nothing as a principle that has not yet been thoroughly proved from phenomena. They do not contrive hypotheses, nor do they admit them into natural science otherwise than as questions whose truth may be discussed. Therefore they proceed by a twofold method, analytic and synthetic. From certain selected phenomena they deduce by analysis the forces of nature and the simpler laws of those forces, from which they then give the constitution of the rest of the phenomena by synthesis. This is that incomparably best way of philosophizing which our most celebrated author thought should be justly embraced in preference to all others. This alone he judged worthy of being cultivated and enriched by the expenditure of his labor. Of this therefore he has given a most illustrious example, namely, the explication of the system of the world most successfully deduced from the theory of gravity. That the force of gravity is in all bodies universally, others have suspected or imagined; Newton was the first and only one who was able to demonstrate it from phenomena and to make it a solid foundation for his brilliant theories.

I know indeed that some men, even of great reputation, unduly influenced by certain prejudices, have found it difficult to accept this new principle and have repeatedly preferred uncertainties to certainties. It is not my intention to carp at their reputation; rather, I wish to give you in brief, kind reader, the basis for making a fair judgment of the issue for yourself.

Therefore, to begin our discussion with what is simplest and nearest to us, let us briefly consider what the nature of gravity is in terrestrial bodies, so that when we come to consider celestial bodies, so very far removed from us, we may proceed more securely. It is now agreed among all philosophers that all bodies on or near the earth universally gravitate toward the earth. Manifold experience has long confirmed that there are no truly light bodies. What is called relative levity is not true levity, but only apparent, and arises from the more powerful gravity of contiguous bodies.

Furthermore, just as all bodies universally gravitate toward the earth, so the earth in turn gravitates equally toward the bodies; for the action of gravity is mutual and is equal in both directions. This is shown as follows. Let the whole body of the earth be divided into any two parts, whether equal or in any way unequal; now, if the weights of the parts toward each other were not equal, the lesser weight would yield to the greater, and the parts, joined together, would proceed to move straight on without limit in the direction toward which the greater weight tends, entirely contrary to experience. Therefore the necessary conclusion is that the weights of the parts are in equilibrium – that is, that the action of gravity is mutual and equal in both directions.

The weights of bodies equally distant from the center of the earth are as the quantities of matter in the bodies. This is gathered from the equal acceleration of all bodies falling from rest by the force of their weights; for the forces by which unequal bodies are equally accelerated must be proportional to the quantities of matter to be moved. Now, that all falling bodies universally are equally accelerated is evident from this, that in the vacuum produced by Boyle's air pump (that is, with the resistance of the air removed), they describe, in falling, equal spaces in equal times, and this is proved more exactly by experiments with pendulums.

The attractive forces of bodies, at equal distances, are as the quantities of matter in the bodies. For, since bodies gravitate toward the earth, and the earth in turn gravitates toward the bodies, with equal moments [i.e. strengths or powers], the weight of the earth toward each body, or the force by which the body attracts the earth, will be equal to the weight of the body toward the earth. But, as mentioned above, this weight is as the quantity of matter in the body, and so the force by which each body attracts the earth, or the absolute force of the body, will be as its quantity of matter.

Therefore the attractive force of entire bodies arises and is compounded from the attractive force of the parts, since (as has been shown), when the amount of matter is increased or diminished, its force is proportionally increased or diminished. Therefore the action of the earth must result from the combined actions of its parts; hence all terrestrial bodies must attract one another by absolute forces that are proportional to the attracting matter. This is the nature of gravity on earth; let us now see what it is in the heavens.

Every body perseveres in its state either of being at rest or of moving uniformly straight forward, except insofar as it is compelled by impressed forces to change that state: this is a law of nature accepted by all philosophers. It follows that bodies that move in curves, and so continually deviate from straight lines tangent to their orbits, are kept in a curvilinear path by some continually acting force. Therefore, for the planets to revolve in curved orbits, there will necessarily be some force by whose repeated actions they are unceasingly deflected from the tangents.

Now, it is reasonable to accept something that can be found by mathematics and proved with the greatest certainty: namely, that all bodies moving in some curved line described in a plane, which by a radius drawn to a point (either at rest or moving in any way) describe areas about that point proportional to the times, are urged by forces that tend toward that same point. Therefore, since it is agreed among astronomers that the primary planets describe areas around the sun proportional to the times, as do the secondary planets around their own primary planets, it follows that the force by which they are continually pulled away from rectilinear tangents and are compelled to revolve in curvilinear orbits is directed toward the bodies that are situated in the centers of the orbits. Therefore this force can, appropriately, be called centripetal with respect to the revolving body, and attractive with respect to the central body, from whatever cause it may in the end be imagined to arise.

The following rules must also be accepted and are mathematically demonstrated. If several bodies revolve with uniform motion in concentric circles, and if the squares of the periodic times are as the cubes of the distances from the common center, then the centripetal forces of the revolving bodies will be inversely as the squares of the distances. Again, if the bodies revolve in orbits that are very nearly circles, and if the apsides of the orbits are at rest, then the centripetal forces of the revolving bodies will be inversely as the squares of the distances. Astronomers agree that one or the other case holds for all the planets [both primary and secondary]. Therefore the centripetal forces of all the planets are inversely as the squares of the distances from the centers of the orbits. If anyone objects that the apsides of the planets, especially the apsides of the moon, are not completely at rest but are carried progressively forward [or in consequentia] with a slow motion, it can be answered that even if we grant that this very slow motion arises from a slight deviation of the centripetal force from the proportion of the inverse square, this difference can be found by mathematical computation and is quite insensible. For the ratio of the moon's centripetal force itself, which should deviate most of all from the square, will indeed exceed the square by a very little, but it will be about sixty times closer to it than to the cube. But our answer to the objection will be truer if we say that this progression of the apsides does not arise from a deviation from the proportion of the [inverse] square but from another and entirely different cause, as is admirably shown in Newton's philosophy. As a result, the centripetal forces by which the primary planets tend toward the sun, and the secondary planets toward their primaries, must be exactly as the squares of the distances inversely.

From what has been said up to this point, it is clear that the planets are kept in their orbits by some force continually acting upon them, that this force is always directed toward the centers of the orbits, and that its efficacy is increased in approaching the center and decreased in receding from the center – actually increased in the same proportion in which the square of the distance is decreased, and decreased in the same proportion in which the square of the distance is increased. Let us now, by comparing the centripetal forces of the planets and the force of gravity, see whether or not they might be of the same kind. They will be of the same kind if the same laws and the same attributes are found in both. Let us first, therefore, consider the centripetal force of the moon, which is closest to us.

When bodies are let fall from rest, and are acted on by any forces whatever, the rectilinear spaces described in a given time at the very beginning of the motion are proportional to the forces themselves; this of course follows from mathematical reasoning. Therefore the centripetal force of the moon revolving in its orbit will be to the force of gravity on the earth's surface as the space that the moon would describe in a minimally small time in descending toward the earth by its centripetal force – supposing it to be deprived of all circular motion – is to the space that a heavy body describes in the same minimally small time in the vicinity of the earth, in falling by the force of its own gravity. The first of these spaces is equal to the versed sine of the arc described by the moon during the same time, inasmuch as this versed sine measures the departure of the moon from the tangent caused by centripetal force and thus can be calculated if the moon's periodic time and its distance from the center of the earth are both given. The second space is found by experiments with pendulums, as Huygens has shown. Therefore, the result of the calculation will be that the first space is to the second space, or the centripetal force of the moon revolving in its orbit is to the force of gravity on the surface of the earth, as the square of the semidiameter of the earth is to the square of the semidiameter of the orbit. By what is shown above, the same ratio holds for the centripetal force of the moon revolving in its orbit and the centripetal force of the moon if it were near the earth's surface. Therefore this centripetal force near the earth's surface is equal to the force of gravity. They are not, therefore, different forces, but one and the same; for if they were different, bodies acted on by both forces together would fall to the earth twice as fast as from the force of gravity alone. And therefore it is clear that this centripetal force by which the moon is continually either drawn or impelled from the tangent and is kept in its orbit is the very force of terrestrial gravity extending as far as the moon. And indeed it is reasonable for this force to extend itself to enormous distances, since one can observe no sensible diminution of it even on the highest peaks of mountains. Therefore the moon gravitates toward the earth. Further, by mutual action, the earth in turn gravitates equally toward the moon, a fact which is abundantly confirmed in this philosophy, when we deal with the tide of the sea and the precession of the equinoxes, both of which arise from the action of both the moon and the sun upon the earth. Hence finally we learn also by what law the force of gravity decreases at greater distances from the earth. For since gravity is not different from the moon's centripetal force, which is inversely proportional to the square of the distance, gravity will also be diminished in the same ratio.

Let us now proceed to the other planets. The revolutions of the primary planets about the sun and of the secondary planets about Jupiter and Saturn are phenomena of the same kind as the revolution of the moon about the earth; furthermore, it has been demonstrated that the centripetal forces of the primary planets are directed toward the center of the sun, and those of the secondary planets toward the centers of Jupiter and of Saturn, just as the moon's centripetal force is directed toward the center of the earth; and, additionally, all these forces are inversely as the squares of the distances from the centers, just as the force of the moon is inversely as the square of the distance from the earth. Therefore it must be concluded that all of these primary and secondary planets have the same nature. Hence, as the moon gravitates toward the earth, and the earth in turn gravitates toward the moon, so also all the secondary planets will gravitate toward their primaries, and the primaries in turn toward the secondaries, and also all the primary planets will gravitate toward the sun, and the sun in turn toward the primary planets.

Therefore the sun gravitates toward all the primary and secondary planets, and all these toward the sun. For the secondary planets, while accompanying their primaries, revolve with them around the sun. By the same argument, therefore, both kinds of planets gravitate toward the sun, and the sun toward them. Additionally, that the secondary planets gravitate toward the sun is also abundantly clear from the inequalities of the moon, concerning which a most exact theory is presented with marvelous sagacity in the third book of this work.

The motion of the comets shows very clearly that the attractive force of the sun is propagated in every direction to enormous distances and is diffused to every part of the surrounding space, since the comets, starting out from immense distances, come into the vicinity of the sun and sometimes approach so very close to it that in their perihelia they all seemingly touch its globe. Astronomers until now have tried in vain to find the theory of these comets; now at last, in our time, our most illustrious author has succeeded in finding the theory and has demonstrated it with the greatest certainty from observations. It is therefore evident that the comets move in conic sections having their foci in the center of the sun and by radii drawn to the sun describe areas proportional to the times. From these phenomena it is manifest and it is mathematically proved that the forces by which the comets are kept in their orbits are directed toward the sun and are inversely as the squares of their distances from its center. Thus the comets gravitate toward the sun; and so the attractive force of the sun reaches not only to the bodies of the planets, which are at fixed distances and in nearly the same plane, but also to the comets, which are in the most diverse regions of the heavens and at the most diverse distances. It is the nature of gravitating bodies, therefore, that they propagate their forces at all distances to all other gravitating bodies. From this it follows that all planets and comets universally attract one another and are heavy toward one another – which is also confirmed by the perturbation of Jupiter and Saturn, known to astronomers and arising from the actions of these planets upon each other; it is also confirmed by the very slow motion of the apsides that was mentioned above and that arises from an entirely similar cause.

We have at last reached the point where it must be acknowledged that the earth and the sun and all the celestial bodies that accompany the sun attract one another. Therefore every least particle of each of them will have its own attractive force in proportion to the quantity of matter, as was shown above for terrestrial bodies. And at different distances their forces will also be in the squared ratio of the distances inversely; for it is mathematically demonstrated that particles attracting by this law must constitute globes attracting by the same law.

The preceding conclusions are based upon an axiom which is accepted by every philosopher, namely, that effects of the same kind – that is, effects whose known properties are the same – have the same causes, and their properties which are not yet known are also the same. For if gravity is the cause of the fall of a stone in Europe, who can doubt that in America the cause of the fall is the same? If gravity is mutual between a stone and the earth in Europe, who will deny that it is mutual in America? If in Europe the attractive force of the stone and the earth is compounded of the attractive forces of the parts, who will deny that in America the force is similarly compounded? If in Europe the attraction of the earth is propagated to all kinds of bodies and to all distances, why should we not say that in America it is propagated in the same way? All philosophy is based on this rule, inasmuch as, if it is taken away, there is then nothing we can affirm about things universally. The constitution of individual things can be found by observations and experiments; and proceeding from there, it is only by this rule that we make judgments about the nature of things universally.

Now, since all terrestrial and celestial bodies on which we can make experiments or observations are heavy, it must be acknowledged without exception that gravity belongs to all bodies universally. And just as we must not conceive of bodies that are not extended, mobile, and impenetrable, so we should not conceive of any that are not heavy. The extension, mobility, and impenetrability of bodies are known only through experiments; it is in exactly the same way that the gravity of bodies is known. All bodies for which we have observations are extended and mobile and impenetrable; and from this we conclude that all bodies universally are extended and mobile and impenetrable, even those for which we do not have observations. Thus all bodies for which we have observations are heavy; and from this we conclude that all bodies universally are heavy, even those for which we do not have observations. If anyone were to say that the bodies of the fixed stars are not heavy, since their gravity has not yet been observed, then by the same argument one would be able to say that they are neither extended nor mobile nor impenetrable, since these properties of the fixed stars have not yet been observed. Need I go on? Among the primary qualities of all bodies universally, either gravity will have a place, or extension, mobility, and impenetrability will not. And the nature of things either will be correctly explained by the gravity of bodies or will not be correctly explained by the extension, mobility, and impenetrability of bodies.

I can hear some people disagreeing with this conclusion and muttering something or other about occult qualities. They are always prattling on and on to the effect that gravity is something occult, and that occult causes are to be banished completely from philosophy. But it is easy to answer them: occult causes are not those causes whose existence is very clearly demonstrated by observations, but only those whose existence is occult, imagined, and not yet proved. Therefore gravity is not an occult cause of celestial motions, since it has been shown from phenomena that this force really exists.[1] Rather, occult causes are the refuge of those who assign the governing of these motions to some sort of vortices of a certain matter utterly fictitious and completely imperceptible to the senses.

But will gravity be called an occult cause and be cast out of natural philosophy on the grounds that the cause of gravity itself is occult and not yet found? Let those who so believe take care lest they believe in an absurdity that, in the end, may overthrow the foundations of all philosophy. For causes generally proceed in a continuous chain from compound to more simple; when you reach the simplest cause, you will not be able to proceed any further. Therefore no mechanical explanation can be given for the simplest cause; for if it could, the cause would not yet be the simplest. Will you accordingly call these simplest causes occult, and banish them? But at the same time the causes most immediately depending on them, and the causes that in turn depend on these causes, will also be banished, until philosophy is emptied and thoroughly purged of all causes.

Some say that gravity is preternatural and call it a perpetual miracle.[2] Therefore they hold that it should be rejected, since preternatural causes have no place in physics. It is hardly worth spending time on demolishing this utterly absurd objection, which of itself undermines all of philosophy. For either they will say that gravity is not a property of all bodies – which cannot be maintained – or they will assert that gravity is preternatural on the grounds that it does not arise from other affections of bodies and thus not from mechanical causes. Certainly there are primary affections of bodies, and since they are primary, they do not depend on others. Therefore let them consider whether or not all these are equally preternatural,

[1] Newton makes the same claim in the General Scholium to the *Principia*, reprinted in this volume (p. 92).
[2] See Leibniz's 1712 letter to Hartsoeker, printed in the *Memoirs of Literature*, and reprinted in this volume (p. 113).

and so equally to be rejected, and let them consider what philosophy will then be like.

There are some who do not like all this celestial physics just because it seems to be in conflict with the doctrines of Descartes and seems scarcely capable of being reconciled with these doctrines. They are free to enjoy their own opinion, but they ought to act fairly and not deny to others the same liberty that they demand for themselves. Therefore, we should be allowed to adhere to the Newtonian philosophy, which we consider truer, and to prefer causes proved by phenomena to causes imagined and not yet proved. It is the province of true philosophy to derive the natures of things from causes that truly exist, and to seek those laws by which the supreme artificer willed to establish this most beautiful order of the world, not those laws by which he could have, had it so pleased him. For it is in accord with reason that the same effect can arise from several causes somewhat different from one another; but the true cause will be the one from which the effect truly and actually does arise, while the rest have no place in true philosophy. In mechanical clocks one and the same motion of the hour hand can arise from the action of a suspended weight or an internal spring. But if the clock under discussion is really activated by a weight, then anyone will be laughed at if he imagines a spring and on such a premature hypothesis undertakes to explain the motion of the hour hand; for he ought to have examined the internal workings of the machine more thoroughly, in order to ascertain the true principle of the motion in question. The same judgment or something like it should be passed on those philosophers who have held that the heavens are filled with a certain most subtle matter, which is endlessly moved in vortices. For even if these philosophers could account for the phenomena with the greatest exactness on the basis of their hypotheses, still they cannot be said to have given us a true philosophy and to have found the true causes of the celestial motions until they have demonstrated either that these causes really do exist or at least that others do not exist. Therefore if it can be shown that the attraction of all bodies universally has a true place in the nature of things, and if it further can be shown how all the celestial motions are solved by that attraction, then it would be an empty and ridiculous objection if anyone said that those motions should be explained by vortices, even if we gave our fullest assent to the possibility of such an explanation.[3] But we

---

[3] See Newton's 1693 letter to Leibniz, reprinted in this volume (pp. 108–9).

do not give our assent; for the phenomena can by no means be explained by vortices, as our author fully proves with the clearest arguments. It follows that those who devote their fruitless labor to patching up a most absurd figment of their imagination and embroidering it further with new fabrications must be overly indulging their fantasies.

If the bodies of the planets and the comets are carried around the sun by vortices, the bodies carried around must move with the same velocity and in the same direction as the immediately surrounding parts of the vortices, and must have the same density or the same force of inertia in proportion to the bulk of the matter. But it is certain that planets and comets, while they are in the same regions of the heavens, move with a variety of velocities and directions. Therefore it necessarily follows that those parts of the celestial fluid that are at the same distances from the sun revolve in the same time in different directions with different velocities; for there will be need of one direction and velocity to permit the planets to move through the heavens, and another for the comets. Since this cannot be accounted for, either it will have to be confessed that all the celestial bodies are not carried by the matter of a vortex, or it will have to be said that their motions are to be derived not from one and the same vortex, but from more than one, differing from one another and going through the same space surrounding the sun.

If it is supposed that several vortices are contained in the same space and penetrate one another and revolve with different motions, then – since these motions must conform to the motions of the bodies being carried around, motions highly regular in conic sections that are sometimes extremely eccentric and sometimes very nearly circular – it will be right to ask how it can happen that these same vortices keep their integrity without being in the least perturbed through so many centuries by the interactions of their matter. Surely, if these imaginary motions are more complex and more difficult to explain than the true motions of the planets and comets, I think it pointless to admit them into natural philosophy; for every cause must be simpler than its effect. Granted the freedom to invent any fiction, let someone assert that all the planets and comets are surrounded by atmospheres, as our earth is, a hypothesis that will certainly seem more reasonable than the hypothesis of vortices. Let him then assert that these atmospheres, of their own nature, move around the sun and describe conic sections, a motion that can surely be much more easily conceived than the similar motion of vortices penetrating one another.

Finally, let him maintain that it must be believed that the planets themselves and the comets are carried around the sun by their atmospheres, and
let him celebrate his triumph for having found the causes of the celestial
motions. Anyone who thinks that this fiction should be rejected will also
reject the other one; for the hypothesis of atmospheres and the hypothesis
of vortices are as alike as two peas in a pod.

Galileo showed that when a stone is projected and moves in a parabola,
its deflection from a rectilinear path arises from the gravity of the stone
toward the earth, that is, from an occult quality. Nevertheless it can happen
that some other philosopher, even more clever, may contrive another
cause. He will accordingly imagine that a certain subtle matter, which is
not perceived by sight or by touch or by any of the senses, is found in
the regions that are most immediately contiguous to the surface of the
earth. He will argue, moreover, that this matter is carried in different
directions by various and – for the most part – contrary motions and that
it describes parabolic curves. Finally he will beautifully show how the
stone is deflected and will earn the applause of the crowd. The stone, says
he, floats in that subtle fluid and, by following the course of that fluid,
cannot but describe the same path. But the fluid moves in parabolic curves;
therefore the stone must move in a parabola. Who will not now marvel
at the most acute genius of this philosopher, brilliantly deducing the
phenomena of nature from mechanical causes – at a level comprehensible
even to ordinary people! Who indeed will not jeer at that poor Galileo,
who undertook by a great mathematical effort once more to bring back
occult qualities, happily excluded from philosophy! But I am ashamed to
waste any more time on such trifles.

It all finally comes down to this: the number of comets is huge; their
motions are highly regular and observe the same laws as the motions of the
planets. They move in conic orbits; these orbits are very, very eccentric.
Comets go everywhere into all parts of the heavens and pass very freely
through the regions of the planets, often contrary to the order of the
signs. These phenomena are confirmed with the greatest certainty by
astronomical observations and cannot be explained by vortices. Further,
these phenomena are even inconsistent with planetary vortices. There
will be no room at all for the motions of the comets unless that imaginary
matter is completely removed from the heavens.

For if the planets are carried around the sun by vortices those parts of
the vortices that most immediately surround each planet will be of the

same density as the planet, as has been said above. Therefore all the matter that is contiguous to the perimeter of the earth's orbit will have the same density as the earth, while all the matter that lies between the earth's orbit and the orbit of Saturn will have either an equal or a greater density. For, in order that the constitution of a vortex may be able to last, the less dense parts must occupy the centre, and the more dense parts must be further away from the centre. For since the periodic times of the planets are as the powers of the distances from the sun, the periods of the parts of the vortex should keep the same ratio. It follows that the centrifugal forces of these parts will be inversely as the squares of the distances. Therefore those parts that are at a greater distance from the center strive to recede from it by a smaller force; accordingly, if they should be less dense, it would be necessary for them to yield to the greater force by which the parts nearer to the center endeavor to ascend. Therefore the denser parts will ascend, the less dense will descend, and a mutual exchange of places will occur, until the fluid matter of the whole vortex has been arranged in such order that it can now rest in equilibrium [i.e. its parts are completely at rest with respect to one another or no longer have any motion of ascent or descent]. If two fluids of different density are contained in the same vessel, certainly it will happen that the fluid whose density is greater will go to the lowest place under the action of its greater force of gravity, and by similar reasoning it must be concluded that the denser parts of the vortex will go to the highest place under the action of their greater centrifugal force. Therefore the whole part of the vortex that lies outside the earth's orbit (much the greatest part) will have a density and so a force of inertia (proportional to the quantity of matter) that will not be smaller than the density and force of inertia of the earth. From this will arise a huge and very noticeable resistance to the comets as they pass through, not to say a resistance that rightly seems to be able to put a complete stop to their motion and absorb it entirely. It is however clear from the altogether regular motion of comets that they encounter no resistance that can be in the least perceived, and thus that they do not come upon any matter that has any force of resistance, or accordingly that has any density or force of inertia. For the resistance of mediums arises either from the inertia of fluid matter or from its friction. That which arises from friction is extremely slight and indeed can scarcely be observed in commonly known fluids, unless they are very tenacious like oil and honey. The resistance that is encountered in air, water, quicksilver, and non-tenacious fluids of this sort is almost wholly of the first kind and cannot be decreased in subtlety by any further degree, if the fluid's density or force of inertia – to which this resistance is always proportional – remains the same. This is most clearly demonstrated by our author in his brilliant theory of the resistance of fluids, which in this second edition is presented in a somewhat more accurate manner and is more fully confirmed by experiments with falling bodies.

As bodies move forward, they gradually communicate their motion to a surrounding fluid, and by communicating their motion lose it, and by losing it are retarded. Therefore the retardation is proportional to the motion so communicated, and the motion communicated (where the velocity of the moving body is given) is as the density of the fluid; therefore the retardation or resistance will also be as the density of the fluid and cannot be removed by any means unless the fluid, returning to the back of the body, restores the lost motion. But this cannot be the case unless the force of the fluid on the rear of the body is equal to the force the body exerts on the fluid in front, that is, unless the relative velocity with which the fluid pushes the body from behind is equal to the velocity with which the body pushes the fluid, that is, unless the absolute velocity of the returning fluid is twice as great as the absolute velocity of the fluid pushed forward, which cannot happen. Therefore there is no way in which the resistance of fluids that arises from their density and force of inertia can be taken away. And so it must be concluded that the celestial fluid has no force of inertia, since it has no force of resistance; it has no force by which motion may be communicated, since it has no force of inertia; it has no force by which any change may be introduced into one or more bodies, since it has no force by which motion may be communicated; it has no efficacy at all, since it has no faculty to introduce any change. Surely, therefore, this hypothesis, plainly lacking in any foundation and not even marginally useful to explain the nature of things, may well be called utterly absurd and wholly unworthy of a philosopher. Those who hold that the heavens are filled with fluid matter, but suppose this matter to have no inertia, are saying there is no vacuum but in fact are assuming there is one. For, since there is no way to distinguish a fluid matter of this sort from empty space, the whole argument comes down to the names of things and not their natures. But if anyone is so devoted to matter that he will in no way admit a space void of bodies, let us see where this will ultimately lead him.

For such people will say that this constitution of the universe as everywhere full, which is how they imagine it, has arisen from the will of God,
so that a very subtle aether pervading and filling all things would be there
to facilitate the operations of nature; this cannot be maintained, however,
since it has already been shown from the phenomena of comets that this
aether has no efficacy. Or they will say that this constitution has arisen
from the will of God for some unknown purpose, which ought not to be
said either, since a different constitution of the universe could equally well
be established by the same argument. Or finally they will say that it has
not arisen from the will of God but from some necessity of nature. And so
at last they must sink to the lowest depths of degradation, where they have
the fantasy that all things are governed by fate and not by providence,
that matter has existed always and everywhere of its own necessity and
is infinite and eternal. On this supposition, matter will also be uniform
everywhere, for variety of forms is entirely inconsistent with necessity.
Matter will also be without motion; for if by necessity matter moves in
some definite direction with some definite velocity, by a like necessity it
will move in a different direction with a different velocity; but it cannot
move in different directions with different velocities; therefore it must be
without motion. Surely, this world – so beautifully diversified in its forms
and motions – could not have arisen except from the perfectly free will of
God, who provides and governs all things.

From this source, then, have all the laws that are called laws of nature
come, in which many traces of the highest wisdom and counsel certainly
appear, but no traces of necessity. Accordingly we should not seek these
laws by using untrustworthy conjectures, but learn them by observing and
experimenting. He who is confident that he can truly find the principles
of physics, and the laws of things, by relying only on the force of his
mind and the internal light of his reason[4] should maintain either that
the world has existed from necessity and follows the said laws from the
same necessity, or that although the order of nature was constituted by
the will of God, nevertheless a creature as small and insignificant as he
is has a clear understanding of the way things should be. All sound and
true philosophy is based on phenomena, which may lead us – however
unwilling and reluctant – to principles in which the best counsel and
highest dominion of an all-wise and all-powerful being are most clearly

---

[4] This is intended as a criticism of Descartes' procedure in the *Principles of Philosophy*.

discerned; these principles will not be rejected because certain men may perhaps not like them. These men may call the things that they dislike either miracles or occult qualities, but names maliciously given are not to be blamed on the things themselves, unless these men are willing to confess at last that philosophy should be based on atheism. Philosophy must not be overthrown for their sake, since the order of things refuses to be changed.

Therefore honest and fair judges will approve the best method of natural philosophy, which is based on experiments and observations. It need scarcely be said that this way of philosophizing has been illumined and dignified by our illustrious author's well-known book; his tremendous genius, enodating [clarifying or solving] each of the most difficult problems and reaching out beyond the accepted limits of the human, is justly admired and esteemed by all who are more than superficially versed in these matters. Having unlocked the gates, therefore, he has opened our way to the most beautiful mysteries of nature. He has finally so clearly revealed a most elegant structure of the system of the world for our further scrutiny that even were King Alfonso himself to come to life again, he would not find it wanting either in simplicity or in grace of harmony.[5] And hence it is now possible to have a closer view of the majesty of nature, to enjoy the sweetest contemplation, and to worship and venerate more zealously the maker and lord of all; and this is by far the greatest fruit of philosophy. He must be blind who does not at once see, from the best and wisest structures of things, the infinite wisdom and goodness of their almighty creator; and he must be mad who refuses to acknowledge them.

Therefore Newton's excellent treatise will stand as a mighty fortress against the attacks of atheists; nowhere else will you find more effective ammunition against that impious crowd. This was understood long ago, and was first splendidly demonstrated in learned discourses in English and in Latin, by a man of universal learning and at the same time an outstanding patron of the arts, Richard Bentley, a great ornament of his time and of our academy, the worthy and upright master

---

[5] Alfonso X, the Spanish King of Castile and Leon (1252–82), compiled the so-called Alfonsine Tables in astronomy, and was reputed to have claimed that if he had been given a few simple principles he could have created a simpler system of the world than that depicted by then-current Ptolemaic astronomy.

of our Trinity College.[6] I must confess that I am indebted to him on many grounds; you as well, kind reader, will not deny him due thanks. For, as a long-time intimate friend of our renowned author (he considers being celebrated by posterity for this friendship to be of no less value than becoming famous for his own writings, which are the delight of the learned world), he worked simultaneously for the public recognition of his friend and for the advancement of the sciences. Therefore, since the available copies of the first edition were extremely rare and very expensive, he tried with persistent demands to persuade Newton (who is distinguished as much by modesty as by the highest learning) and finally – almost scolding him – prevailed upon Newton to allow him to get out this new edition, under his auspices and at his own expense, perfected throughout and also enriched with significant additions. He authorized me to undertake the not unpleasant duty of seeing to it that all this was done as correctly as possible.

Cambridge, 12 May 1713
Roger Cotes, Fellow of Trinity College, Plumian Professor of Astronomy and Experimental Philosophy

Definitions

Definition 1

Quantity of matter is a measure of matter that arises from its density and volume jointly.

If the density of air is doubled in a space that is also doubled, there is four times as much air, and there is six times as much if the space is tripled. The case is the same for snow and powders condensed by compression or liquefaction, and also for all bodies that are condensed in various ways by any causes whatsoever. For the present, I am not taking into account any medium, if there should be any, freely pervading the interstices between the parts of bodies. Furthermore, I mean this quantity whenever I use the term 'body' or 'mass' in the following pages. It can always be known from a body's weight, for – by making very accurate experiments with pendulums – I have found it to be proportional to the weight, as will be shown below.

---

[6] See Newton's letters to Bentley in this volume.

Definition 2

Quantity of motion is a measure of motion that arises from the velocity and the quantity of matter jointly.

The motion of a whole is the sum of the motions of the individual parts, and thus if a body is twice as large as another and has equal velocity there is twice as much motion, and if it has twice the velocity there is four times as much motion.

Definition 3

Inherent force of matter is the power of resisting by which every body, so far as it is able, perseveres in its state either of resting or of moving uniformly straight forward.

This force is always proportional to the body and does not differ in any way from the inertia of the mass except in the manner in which it is conceived. Because of the inertia of matter, every body is only with difficulty put out of its state either of resting or of moving. Consequently, inherent force may also be called by the very significant name of force of inertia. Moreover, a body exerts this force only during a change of its state, caused by another force impressed upon it, and this exercise of force is, depending on the viewpoint, both resistance and impetus: resistance insofar as the body, in order to maintain its state, strives against the impressed force, and impetus insofar as the same body, yielding only with difficulty to the force of a resisting obstacle, endeavors to change the state of that obstacle. Resistance is commonly attributed to resting bodies and impetus to moving bodies; but motion and rest, in the popular sense of the terms, are distinguished from each other only by point of view, and bodies commonly regarded as being at rest are not always truly at rest.

Definition 4

Impressed force is the action exerted on a body to change its state either of resting or of moving uniformly straight forward.

This force consists solely in the action and does not remain in a body after the action has ceased. For a body perseveres in any new state solely by the force of inertia. Moreover, there are various sources of impressed force, such as percussion, pressure, or centripetal force.

Definition 5

Centripetal force is the force by which bodies are drawn from all sides, are impelled, or in any way tend, toward some point as to a center.

One force of this kind is gravity, by which bodies tend toward the center of the earth; another is magnetic force, by which iron seeks a lodestone; and yet another is that force, whatever it may be, by which the planets are continually drawn back from rectilinear motions and compelled to revolve around curved lines. A stone whirled in a sling endeavors to leave the hand that is whirling it, and by its endeavor it stretches the sling, doing so the more strongly the more swiftly it revolves; and as soon as it is released, it flies away. The force opposed to that endeavor, that is, the force by which the sling continually draws the stone back toward the hand and keeps it in an orbit, I call centripetal, since it is directed toward the hand as toward the center of an orbit. And the same applies to all bodies that are made to move in orbits. They all endeavor to recede from the centers of their orbits, and unless some force opposed to that endeavor is present, restraining them and keeping them in orbits and hence called by me centripetal, they will go off in straight lines with uniform motion. If a projectile were deprived of the force of gravity, it would not be deflected toward the earth but would go off in a straight line into the heavens and do so with uniform motion, provided that the resistance of the air were removed. The projectile, by its gravity, is drawn back from a rectilinear course and continually deflected toward the earth, and this is so to a greater or lesser degree in proportion to its gravity and its velocity of motion. The less its gravity in proportion to its quantity of matter, or the greater the velocity with which it is projected, the less it will deviate from a rectilinear course and the farther it will go. If a lead ball were projected with a given velocity along a horizontal line from the top of some mountain by the force of gunpowder and went in a curved line for a distance of two miles before falling to the earth, then the same ball projected with twice the velocity would go about twice as far and with ten times the velocity about ten times as far, provided that the resistance of the air were removed. And by increasing the velocity, the distance to which it would be projected could be increased at will and the curvature of the line that it would describe could be decreased, in such a way that it would finally fall at a distance of 10 or 30 or 90 degrees or even go around the whole earth or, lastly, go off into the heavens and continue indefinitely in this motion. And in the same way that a projectile could, by the force of gravity, be deflected into an orbit and go around the whole earth, so too the moon, whether by the force of gravity – if it has gravity – or by any other force by which it may be urged toward the earth, can always be drawn back toward the earth from a rectilinear course and deflected into its orbit; and without such a force the moon cannot be kept in its orbit. If this force were too small, it would not deflect the moon sufficiently from a rectilinear course; if it were too great, it would deflect the moon excessively and draw it down from its orbit toward the earth. In fact, it must be of just the right magnitude, and mathematicians have the task of finding the force by which a body can be kept exactly in any given orbit with a given velocity and, alternatively, to find the curvilinear path into which a body leaving any given place with a given velocity is deflected by a given force.

The quantity of centripetal force is of three kinds: absolute, accelerative, and motive.

Definition 6

The absolute quantity of centripetal force is the measure of this force that is greater or less in proportion to the efficacy of the cause propagating it from a center through the surrounding regions.

An example is magnetic force, which is greater in one lodestone [i.e. magnet] and less in another, in proportion to the bulk or potency of the lodestone.

Definition 7

The accelerative quantity of centripetal force is the measure of this force that is proportional to the velocity which it generates in a given time.

One example is the potency of a lodestone, which, for a given lodestone, is greater at a smaller distance and less at a greater distance. Another example is the force that produces gravity, which is greater in valleys and less on the peaks of high mountains and still less (as will be made clear below) at greater distances from the body of the earth, but which is everywhere the same at equal distances, because it equally accelerates all falling bodies (heavy or light, great or small), provided that the resistance of the air is removed.

Definition 8

The motive quantity of centripetal force is the measure of this force that is proportional to the motion which it generates in a given time.

An example is weight, which is greater in a larger body and less in a smaller body; and in one and the same body is greater near the earth and less out in the heavens. This quantity is the centripetency, or propensity toward a center, of the whole body, and (so to speak) its weight, and it may always be known from the force opposite and equal to it, which can prevent the body from falling.

These quantities of forces, for the sake of brevity, may be called motive, accelerative, and absolute forces, and, for the sake of differentiation, may be referred to bodies seeking a center, to the places of the bodies, and to the center of the forces: that is, motive force may be referred to a body as an endeavor of the whole directed toward a center and compounded of the endeavors of all the parts; accelerative force, to the place of the body as a certain efficacy diffused from the center through each of the surrounding places in order to move the bodies that are in those places; and absolute force, to the center as having some cause without which the motive forces are not propagated through the surrounding regions, whether this cause is some central body (such as a lodestone in the center of a magnetic force or the earth in the center of a force that produces gravity) or whether it is some other cause which is not apparent. This concept is purely mathematical, for I am not now considering the physical causes and sites of forces.

Therefore, accelerative force is to motive force as velocity to motion. For quantity of motion arises from velocity and quantity of matter jointly, and motive force from accelerative force and quantity of matter jointly. For the sum of the actions of the accelerative force on the individual particles of a body is the motive force of the whole body. As a consequence, near the surface of the earth, where the accelerative gravity, or the force that produces gravity, is the same in all bodies universally, the motive gravity, or weight, is as the body, but in an ascent to regions where the accelerative gravity becomes less, the weight will decrease proportionately and will always be as the body and the accelerative gravity jointly. Thus, in regions where the accelerative gravity is half as great, a body one-half or one-third as great will have a weight four or six times less.

Further, it is in this same sense that I call attractions and impulses accelerative and motive. Moreover, I use interchangeably and indiscriminately words signifying attraction, impulse, or any sort of propensity toward a center, considering these forces not from a physical but only from a mathematical point of view. Therefore, let the reader beware of thinking that by words of this kind I am anywhere defining a species or mode of action or a physical cause or reason, or that I am attributing forces in a true and physical sense to centers (which are mathematical points) if I happen to say that centers attract or that centers have forces.

Scholium

Thus far it has seemed best to explain the senses in which less familiar words are to be taken in this treatise. Although time, space, place, and motion are very familiar to everyone, it must be noted that these quantities are popularly conceived solely with reference to the objects of sense perception. And this is the source of certain preconceptions; to eliminate them it is useful to distinguish these quantities into absolute and relative, true and apparent, mathematical and common.

1. Absolute, true, and mathematical time, in and of itself and of its own nature, without reference to anything external, flows uniformly and by another name is called duration. Relative, apparent, and common time is any sensible and external measure (precise or imprecise) of duration by means of motion; such a measure – for example, an hour, a day, a month, a year – is commonly used instead of true time.

2. Absolute space, of its own nature without reference to anything external, always remains homogeneous and immovable. Relative space is any movable measure or dimension of this absolute space; such a measure or dimension is determined by our senses from the situation of the space with respect to bodies and is popularly used for immovable space, as in the case of space under the earth or in the air or in the heavens, where the dimension is determined from the situation of the space with respect to the earth. Absolute and relative space are the same in species and in magnitude, but they do not always remain the same numerically. For example, if the earth moves, the space of our air, which in a relative sense and with respect to the earth always remains the same, will now be one part of the absolute space into which the air passes, now another part of it, and thus will be changing continually in an absolute sense.

3. Place is the part of space that a body occupies, and it is, depending on the space, either absolute or relative. I say the part of space, not the position of the body or its outer surface. For the places of equal solids are always equal, while their surfaces are for the most part unequal because of the dissimilarity of shapes; and positions, properly speaking, do not have quantity and are not so much places as attributes of places. The motion of a whole is the same as the sum of the motions of the parts; that is, the change in position of a whole from its place is the same as the sum of the changes in position of its parts from their places, and thus the place of a whole is the same as the sum of the places of the parts and therefore is internal and in the whole body.

4. Absolute motion is the change of position of a body from one absolute place to another; relative motion is change of position from one relative place to another. Thus, in a ship under sail, the relative place of a body is that region of the ship in which the body happens to be or that part of the whole interior of the ship which the body fills and which accordingly moves along with the ship, and relative rest is the continuance of the body in that same region of the ship or same part of its interior. But true rest is the continuance of a body in the same part of that unmoving space in which the ship itself, along with its interior and all its contents, is moving. Therefore, if the earth is truly at rest, a body that is relatively at rest on a ship will move truly and absolutely with the velocity with which the ship is moving on the earth. But if the earth is also moving, the true and absolute motion of the body will arise partly from the true motion of the earth in unmoving space and partly from the relative motion of the ship on the earth. Further, if the body is also moving relatively on the ship, its true motion will arise partly from the true motion of the earth in unmoving space and partly from the relative motions both of the ship on the earth and of the body on the ship, and from these relative motions the relative motion of the body on the earth will arise. For example, if that part of the earth where the ship happens to be is truly moving eastward with a velocity of 10,010 units, and the ship is being borne westward by sails and wind with a velocity of 10 units, and a sailor is walking on the ship toward the east with a velocity of 1 unit, then the sailor will be moving truly and absolutely in unmoving space toward the east with a velocity of 10,001 units and relatively on the earth toward the west with a velocity of 9 units.

In astronomy, absolute time is distinguished from relative time by the equation of common time. For natural days, which are commonly considered equal for the purpose of measuring time, are actually unequal. Astronomers correct this inequality in order to measure celestial motions on the basis of a truer time. It is possible that there is no uniform motion by which time may have an exact measure. All motions can be accelerated and retarded, but the flow of absolute time cannot be changed. The duration or perseverance of the existence of things is the same, whether their motions are rapid or slow or null; accordingly, duration is rightly distinguished from its sensible measures and is gathered from them by means of an astronomical equation. Moreover, the need for using this equation in determining when phenomena occur is proved by experience with a pendulum clock and also by eclipses of the satellites of Jupiter.

Just as the order of the parts of time is unchangeable, so, too, is the order of the parts of space. Let the parts of space move from their places, and they will move (so to speak) from themselves. For times and spaces are, as it were, the places of themselves and of all things. All things are placed in time with reference to order of succession and in space with reference to order of position. It is of the essence of spaces to be places, and for primary places to move is absurd. They are therefore absolute places, and it is only changes of position from these places that are absolute motions.

But since these parts of space cannot be seen and cannot be distinguished from one another by our senses, we use sensible measures in their stead. For we define all places on the basis of the positions and distances of things from some body that we regard as immovable, and then we reckon all motions with respect to these places, insofar as we conceive of bodies as being changed in position with respect to them. Thus, instead of absolute places and motions we use relative ones, which is not inappropriate in ordinary human affairs, although in philosophy abstraction from the senses is required. For it is possible that there is no body truly at rest to which places and motions may be referred.

Moreover, absolute and relative rest and motion are distinguished from each other by their properties, causes, and effects. It is a property of rest that bodies truly at rest are at rest in relation to one another. And therefore, since it is possible that some body in the regions of the fixed stars or far beyond is absolutely at rest, and yet it cannot be known from the position of bodies in relation to one another in our regions whether or not any of these maintains a given position with relation to that distant body, true rest cannot be defined on the basis of the position of bodies in relation to one another.[7]

It is a property of motion that parts which keep given positions in relation to wholes participate in the motions of such wholes. For all the parts of bodies revolving in orbit endeavor to recede from the axis of motion, and the impetus of bodies moving forward arises from the joint impetus of the individual parts. Therefore, when bodies containing others move, whatever is relatively at rest within them also moves. And thus true and absolute motion cannot be determined by means of change of position from the vicinity of bodies that are regarded as being at rest. For the exterior bodies ought to be regarded not only as being at rest but also as being truly at rest. Otherwise all contained bodies, besides being subject to change of position from the vicinity of the containing bodies, will participate in the true motions of the containing bodies and, if there is no such change of position, will not be truly at rest but only be regarded as being at rest. For containing bodies are to those inside them as the outer part of the whole to the inner part or as the shell to the kernel. And when the shell moves, the kernel also, without being changed in position from the vicinity of the shell, moves as a part of the whole.

A property akin to the preceding one is that when a place moves, whatever is placed in it moves along with it, and therefore a body moving away from a place that moves participates also in the motion of its place. Therefore, all motions away from places that move are only parts of whole and absolute motions, and every whole motion is compounded of the motion of a body away from its initial place, and the motion of this place away from its place, and so on, until an unmoving place is reached, as in the abovementioned example of the sailor. Thus, whole and absolute motions can be determined only by means of unmoving places, and therefore in what has preceded I have referred such motions to unmoving places and relative motions to movable places. Moreover, the only places that are unmoving are those that all keep given positions in relation to one another from infinity to infinity and therefore always remain immovable and constitute the space that I call immovable.

The causes which distinguish true motions from relative motions are the forces impressed upon bodies to generate motion. True motion is

[7] This is intended as a criticism of Descartes; cf. the extended discussion in *De Gravitatione* in this volume.

neither generated nor changed except by forces impressed upon the moving body itself, but relative motion can be generated and changed without the impression of forces upon this body. For the impression of forces solely on other bodies with which a given body has a relation is enough, when the other bodies yield, to produce a change in that relation which constitutes the relative rest or motion of this body. Again, true motion is always changed by forces impressed upon a moving body, but relative motion is not necessarily changed by such forces. For if the same forces are impressed upon a moving body and also upon other bodies with which it has a relation, in such a way that the relative position is maintained, the relation that constitutes the relative motion will also be maintained. Therefore, every relative motion can be changed while the true motion is preserved, and can be preserved while the true one is changed, and thus true motion certainly does not consist in relations of this sort.

The effects distinguishing absolute motion from relative motion are the forces of receding from the axis of circular motion. For in purely relative circular motion these forces are null, while in true and absolute circular motion they are larger or smaller in proportion to the quantity of motion. If a bucket is hanging from a very long cord and is continually turned around until the cord becomes twisted tight, and if the bucket is thereupon filled with water and is at rest along with the water and then, by some sudden force, is made to turn around in the opposite direction and, as the cord unwinds, perseveres for a while in this motion; then the surface of the water will at first be level, just as it was before the vessel began to move. But after the vessel, by the force gradually impressed upon the water, has caused the water also to begin revolving perceptibly, the water will gradually recede from the middle and rise up the sides of the vessel, assuming a concave shape (as experience has shown me), and, with an ever faster motion, will rise further and further until, when it completes its revolutions in the same times as the vessel, it is relatively at rest in the vessel. The rise of the water reveals its endeavor to recede from the axis of motion, and from such an endeavor one can find out and measure the true and absolute circular motion of the water, which here is the direct opposite of its relative motion. In the beginning, when the relative motion of the water in the vessel was greatest, that motion was not giving rise to any endeavor to recede from the axis; the water did not seek the circumference by rising up the sides of the vessel but remained level, and therefore its true circular motion had not yet begun.

But afterward, when the relative motion of the water decreased, its rise up the sides of the vessel revealed its endeavor to recede from the axis, and this endeavor showed the true circular motion of the water to be continually increasing and finally becoming greatest when the water was relatively at rest in the vessel. Therefore, that endeavor does not depend on the change of position of the water with respect to surrounding bodies, and thus true circular motion cannot be determined by means of such changes of position. The truly circular motion of each revolving body is unique, corresponding to a unique endeavor as its proper and sufficient effect, while relative motions are innumerable in accordance with their varied relations to external bodies and, like relations, are completely lacking in true effects except insofar as they participate in that true and unique motion. Thus, even in the system of those who hold that our heavens revolve below the heavens of the fixed stars and carry the planets around with them, the individual parts of the heavens, and the planets that are relatively at rest in the heavens to which they belong, are truly in motion. For they change their positions relative to one another (which is not the case with things that are truly at rest), and as they are carried around together with the heavens, they participate in the motions of the heavens and, being parts of revolving wholes, endeavor to recede from the axes of those wholes.

Relative quantities, therefore, are not the actual quantities whose names they bear but are those sensible measures of them (whether true or erroneous) that are commonly used instead of the quantities being measured. But if the meanings of words are to be defined by usage, then it is these sensible measures which should properly be understood by the terms 'time', 'space', 'place', and 'motion', and the manner of expression will be out of the ordinary and purely mathematical if the quantities being measured are understood here. Accordingly those who there interpret these words as referring to the quantities being measured do violence to the Scriptures. And they no less corrupt mathematics and philosophy who confuse true quantities with their relations and common measures.

It is certainly very difficult to find out the true motions of individual bodies and actually to differentiate them from apparent motions, because the parts of that immovable space in which the bodies truly move make no impression on the senses. Nevertheless, the case is not utterly hopeless. For it is possible to draw evidence partly from apparent motions, which are the differences between the true motions, and partly from the forces that are the causes and effects of the true motions. For example, if two balls, at a given distance from each other with a cord connecting them, were revolving about a common center of gravity, the endeavor of the balls to recede from the axis of motion could be known from the tension of the cord, and thus the quantity of circular motion could be computed. Then, if any equal forces were simultaneously impressed upon the alternate faces of the balls to increase or decrease their circular motion, the increase or decrease of the motion could be known from the increased or decreased tension of the cord, and thus, finally, it could be discovered which faces of the balls the forces would have to be impressed upon for a maximum increase in the motion, that is, which were the posterior faces, or the ones that are in the rear in a circular motion. Further, once the faces that follow and the opposite faces that precede were known, the direction of the motion would be known. In this way both the quantity and the direction of this circular motion could be found in any immense vacuum, where nothing external and sensible existed with which the balls could be compared. Now if some distant bodies were set in that space and maintained given positions with respect to one another, as the fixed stars do in the regions of the heavens, it could not, of course, be known from the relative change of position of the balls among the bodies whether the motion was to be attributed to the bodies or to the balls. But if the cord was examined and its tension was discovered to be the very one which the motion of the balls required, it would be valid to conclude that the motion belonged to the balls and that the bodies were at rest, and then, finally, from the change of position of the balls among the bodies, to determine the direction of this motion. But in what follows, a fuller explanation will be given of how to determine true motions from their causes, effects, and apparent differences, and, conversely, of how to determine from motions, whether true or apparent, their causes and effects. For this was the purpose for which I composed the following treatise.

Axioms, or the Laws of Motion

Law I

Every body perseveres in its state of being at rest or of moving uniformly straight forward, except insofar as it is compelled to change its state by forces impressed.

Projectiles persevere in their motions, except insofar as they are retarded by the resistance of the air and are impelled downward by the force of gravity. A spinning hoop, which has parts that by their cohesion continually draw one another back from rectilinear motions, does not cease to rotate, except insofar as it is retarded by the air. And larger bodies – planets and comets – preserve for a longer time both their progressive and their circular motions, which take place in spaces having less resistance.

Law 2

A change in motion is proportional to the motive force impressed and takes place along the straight line in which that force is impressed.

If some force generates any motion, twice the force will generate twice the motion, and three times the force will generate three times the motion, whether the force is impressed all at once or successively by degrees. And if the body was previously moving, the new motion (since motion is always in the same direction as the generative force) is added to the original motion if that motion was in the same direction or is subtracted from the original motion if it was in the opposite direction or, if it was in an oblique direction, is combined obliquely and compounded with it according to the directions of both motions.

Law 3

To any action there is always an opposite and equal reaction; in other words, the actions of two bodies upon each other are always equal and always opposite in direction.

Whatever presses or draws something else is pressed or drawn just as much by it. If anyone presses a stone with a finger, the finger is also pressed by the stone. If a horse draws a stone tied to a rope, the horse will (so to speak) also be drawn back equally toward the stone, for the rope, stretched out at both ends, will urge the horse toward the stone and the stone toward the horse by one and the same endeavor to go slack and will impede the forward motion of the one as much as it promotes the forward motion of the other. If some body impinging upon another body changes the motion of that body in any way by its own force, then, by the force of the other body (because of the equality of their mutual pressure), it also will in turn undergo the same change in its own motion in the opposite direction. By means of these actions, equal changes occur in the motions, not in the velocities – that is, of course, if the bodies are not impeded by anything else. For the changes in velocities that likewise occur in opposite directions are inversely proportional to the bodies because the motions are changed equally. This law is valid also for attractions, as will be proved in the next scholium.

Corollary 1

A body acted on by [two] forces acting jointly describes the diagonal of a parallelogram in the same time in which it would describe the sides if the forces were acting separately.

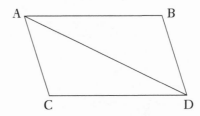

Let a body in a given time, by force M alone impressed in A, be carried with uniform motion from A to B, and, by force N alone impressed in the same place, be carried from A to C; then complete the parallelogram ABDC, and by both forces the body will be carried in the same time along the diagonal from A to D. For, since force N acts along the line AC parallel to BD, this force, by law 2, will make no change at all in the velocity toward the line BD which is generated by the other force. Therefore, the body will reach the line BD in the same time whether force N is impressed or not, and so at the end of that time will be found somewhere on the line BD. By the same argument, at the end of the same time it will be found somewhere on the line CD, and accordingly it is necessarily found at the intersection D of both lines. And, by law 1, it will go with [uniform] rectilinear motion from A to D.

Corollary 2

And hence the composition of a direct force AD out of any oblique forces AB and BD is evident, and conversely the resolution of any direct force AD into any oblique forces AB and BD. And this kind of composition and resolution is indeed abundantly confirmed from mechanics.

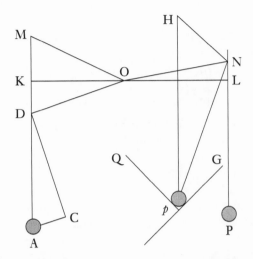

For example, let OM and ON be unequal spokes going out from the center O of any wheel, and let the spokes support the weights A and P by means of the cords MA and NP; it is required to find the forces of the weights to move the wheel. Draw the straight line KOL through the center O, so as to meet the cords perpendicularly at K and L; and with center O and radius OL, which is the greater of OK and OL, describe a circle meeting the cord MA at D; and draw the straight line OD, and let AC be drawn parallel to it and DC perpendicular to it. Since it makes no difference whether points K, L, and D of the cords are attached or not attached to the plane of the wheel, the weights will have the same effect whether they are suspended from the points K and L or from D and L. And if now the total force of the weight A is represented by line AD, it will be resolved into forces [i.e. components] AC and CD, of which AC, drawing spoke OD directly from the center, has no effect in moving the wheel, while the other force DC, drawing spoke DO perpendicularly, has the same effect as if it were drawing spoke OL (equal to OD) perpendicularly; that is, it has the same effect as the weight P, provided that the weight P is to the weight A as the force DC is to the force DA; that is (because triangles ADC and DOK are similar), as OK to OD or OL. Therefore, the weights A and P, which are inversely as the spokes OK and OL (which are in a straight line), will be equipollent and thus will stand in equilibrium, which is a very well known property of the balance, the lever, and the wheel and axle. But if either weight is greater than in this ratio, its force to move the wheel will be so much the greater.

But if the weight p, equal to the weight P, is partly suspended by the cord Np and partly lies on the oblique plane pG, draw pH perpendicular to the plane of the horizon and NH perpendicular to the plane pG; then if the force of the weight p tending downward is represented by the line pH, it can be resolved into the forces [i.e. components] pN and HN. If there were some plane pQ perpendicular to the cord pN and cutting the other plane pG in a line parallel to the horizon, and the weight p were only lying on these planes pQ and pG, the weight p would press these planes perpendicularly with the forces pN and HN – plane pQ, that is, with force pN and plane pG with force HN. Therefore, if the plane pQ is removed, so that the weight stretches the cord, then – since the cord, in sustaining the weight, now takes the place of the plane which has been removed – the cord will be stretched by the same force pN with which the plane was formerly pressed. Thus the tension of this oblique cord will be to the tension of the other, and perpendicular, cord PN as pN to pH. Therefore, if the weight p is to the weight A in a ratio that is compounded of the inverse ratio of the least distances of their respective cords pN and AM from the center of the wheel and the direct ratio of pH to pN, the weights will have the same power to move the wheel and so will sustain each other, as anyone can test.

Now, the weight p, lying on those two oblique planes, has the role of a wedge between the inner surfaces of a body that has been split open; and hence the forces of a wedge and hammer can be determined, because the force with which the weight p presses the plane pQ is to the force with which weight p is impelled along the line pH toward the planes, whether by its own gravity or by the blow of a hammer, as pN is to pH, and because the force with which p presses plane pQ is to the force by which it presses the other plane pG as pN to NH. Furthermore, the force of a screw can also be determined by a similar resolution of forces, inasmuch as it is a wedge impelled by a lever. Therefore, this corollary can be used very extensively, and the variety of its applications clearly shows its truth, since the whole of mechanics – demonstrated in different ways by those who have written on this subject – depends on what has just now been said. For from this are easily derived the forces of machines, which are generally composed of wheels, drums, pulleys, levers, stretched strings, and weights, ascending directly or obliquely, and the other mechanical powers, as well as the forces of tendons to move the bones of animals.

Corollary 3

The quantity of motion, which is determined by adding the motions made in one direction and subtracting the motions made in the opposite direction, is not changed by the action of bodies on one another.

For an action and the reaction opposite to it are equal by law 3, and thus by law 2 the changes which they produce in motions are equal and in opposite directions. Therefore, if motions are in the same direction, whatever is added to the motion of the first body [literally, the fleeing body] will be subtracted from the motion of the second body [literally, the pursuing body] in such a way that the sum remains the same as before. But if the bodies meet head-on, the quantity subtracted from each of the motions will be the same, and thus the difference of the motions made in opposite directions will remain the same.

For example, suppose a spherical body A is three times as large as a spherical body B and has two parts of velocity, and let B follow A in the same straight line with ten parts of velocity; then the motion of A is to the motion of B as six to ten. Suppose that their motions are of six parts and ten parts respectively; the sum will be sixteen parts. When the bodies collide, therefore, if body A gains three or four or five parts of motion, body B will lose just as many parts of motion and thus after reflection body A will continue with nine or ten or eleven parts of motion and B with seven or six or five parts of motion, the sum being always, as originally, sixteen parts of motion. Suppose body A gains nine or ten or eleven or twelve parts of motion and so moves forward with fifteen or sixteen or seventeen or eighteen parts of motion after meeting body B; then body B, by losing as many parts of motion as A gains, will either move forward with one part, having lost nine parts of motion, or will be at rest, having lost its forward motion of ten parts, or will move backward with one part of motion, having lost its motion and (if I may say so) one part more, or will move backward with two parts of motion because a forward motion of twelve parts has been subtracted. And thus the sums, 15 + 1 or 16 + 0, of the motions in the same direction and the differences, 17 − 1 and 18 − 2, of the motions in opposite directions will always be sixteen parts of motion, just as before the bodies met and were reflected. And since the motions with which the bodies will continue to move after reflection are known, the velocity of each will be found, on the supposition that it is to the velocity before reflection as the motion after reflection is to the motion before reflection. For example, in the last case, where the motion of body A was six parts before reflection and eighteen parts afterward, and its velocity was two parts before reflection, its velocity will be found to be six parts after reflection on the basis of the following statement: as six parts of motion before reflection is to eighteen parts of motion afterward, so two parts of velocity before reflection is to six parts of velocity afterward.

But if bodies that either are not spherical or are moving in different straight lines strike against each other obliquely and it is required to find their motions after reflection, the position of the plane by which the colliding bodies are touched at the point of collision must be determined; then (by corollary 2) the motion of each body must be resolved into two motions, one perpendicular to this plane and the other parallel to it. Because the bodies act upon each other along a line perpendicular to this plane, the parallel motions [i.e. components] must be kept the same after reflection; and equal changes in opposite directions must be attributed to the perpendicular motions in such a way that the sum of the motions in the same direction and the difference of the motions in opposite directions remain the same as before the bodies came together. The circular motions of bodies about their own centers also generally arise from reflections of this sort. But I do not consider such cases in what follows, and it would be too tedious to demonstrate everything relating to this subject.

Corollary 4

The common center of gravity of two or more bodies does not change its state whether of motion or of rest as a result of the actions of the bodies upon one another, and therefore the common center of gravity of all bodies acting upon one another (excluding external actions and impediments) either is at rest or moves uniformly straight forward.

For if two points move forward with uniform motion in straight lines, and the distance between them is divided in a given ratio, the dividing point either is at rest or moves forward uniformly in a straight line. This is demonstrated below in lemma 23 and its corollary for the case in which the motions of the points take place in the same plane, and it can be demonstrated by the same reasoning for the case in which those motions do not take place in the same plane. Therefore, if any number of bodies move uniformly in straight lines, the common center of gravity of any two either is at rest or moves forward uniformly in a straight line, because any line joining these bodies through their centers – which move forward uniformly in straight lines – is divided by this common center in a given ratio. Similarly, the common center of gravity of these two bodies and any third body either is at rest or moves forward uniformly in a straight line, because the distance between the common center of the two bodies and the center of the third body is divided in a given ratio by the common center of the three. In the same way, the common center of these three and of any fourth body either is at rest or moves forward uniformly in a straight line, because that common center divides in a given ratio the distance between the common center of the three and the center of the fourth body, and so on without end. Therefore, in a system of bodies in which the bodies are entirely free of actions upon one another and of all other actions impressed upon them externally, and in which each body accordingly moves uniformly in its individual straight line, the common center of gravity of them all either is at rest or moves uniformly straight forward.

Further, in a system of two bodies acting on each other, since the distances of their centers from the common center of gravity are inversely as the bodies, the relative motions of these bodies, whether of approaching that center or of receding from it, will be equal. Accordingly, as a result of equal changes in opposite directions in the motions of these bodies, and consequently as a result of the actions of the bodies on each other, that center is neither accelerated nor retarded nor does it undergo any change in its state of motion or of rest. In a system of several bodies, the common center of gravity of any two acting upon each other does not in any way change its state as a result of that action, and the common center of gravity of the rest of the bodies (with which that action has nothing to do) is not affected by that action; the distance between these two centers is divided by the common center of gravity of all the bodies into parts inversely proportional to the total sums of the bodies whose centers they are, and (since those two centers maintain their state of moving or of being at rest) the common center of all maintains its state also – for all these reasons it is obvious that this common center of all never changes its state with respect to motion and rest as a result of the actions of two bodies upon each other. Moreover, in such a system all the actions of bodies upon one another either occur between two bodies or are compounded of such actions between two bodies and therefore never introduce any change in the state of motion or of rest of the common center of all. Thus, since that center either is at rest or moves forward uniformly in some straight line, when the bodies do not act upon one another, that center will, notwithstanding the actions of the bodies upon one another, continue either to be always at rest or to move always uniformly straight forward, unless it is driven from this state by forces impressed on the system from outside. Therefore, the law is the same for a system of several bodies as for a single body with respect to perseverance in a state of motion or of rest. For the progressive motion, whether of a single body or of a system of bodies, should always be reckoned by the motion of the center of gravity.

Corollary 5

When bodies are enclosed in a given space, their motions in relation to one another are the same whether the space is at rest or whether it is moving uniformly straight forward without circular motion.

For in either case the differences of the motions tending in the same direction and the sums of those tending in opposite directions are the same at the beginning (by hypothesis), and from these sums or differences there arise the collisions and impulses [literally, impetuses] with which the bodies strike one another. Therefore, by law 2, the effects of the collisions will be equal in both cases, and thus the motions with respect to one another in the one case will remain equal to the motions with respect to one another in the other case. This is proved clearly by experience: on a ship, all the motions are the same with respect to one another whether the ship is at rest or is moving uniformly straight forward.

Corollary 6

If bodies are moving in any way whatsoever with respect to one another and are urged by equal accelerative forces along parallel lines, they will all continue to move with respect to one another in the same way as they would if they were not acted on by those forces.

For those forces, by acting equally (in proportion to the quantities of the bodies to be moved) and along parallel lines, will (by law 2) move all the bodies equally (with respect to velocity), and so will never change their positions and motions with respect to one another.

Scholium

The principles I have set forth are accepted by mathematicians and confirmed by experiments of many kinds. By means of the first two laws and the first two corollaries Galileo found that the descent of heavy bodies is in the squared ratio of the time and that the motion of projectiles occurs in a parabola, as experiment confirms, except insofar as these motions are somewhat retarded by the resistance of the air. When a body falls, uniform gravity, by acting equally in individual equal particles of time, impresses equal forces upon that body and generates equal velocities; and in the total time it impresses a total force and generates a total velocity proportional to the time. And the spaces described in proportional times are as the velocities and the times jointly, that is, in the squared ratio of the times. And when a body is projected upward, uniform gravity impresses forces and takes away velocities proportional to the times; and the times of ascending to the greatest heights are as the velocities to be taken away, and these heights are as the velocities and the times jointly, or as the squares of the velocities. And when a body is projected along any straight line, its motion arising from the projection is compounded with the motion arising from gravity.

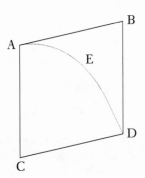

For example, let body A by the motion of projection alone describe the straight line AB in a given time, and by the motion of falling alone describe the vertical distance AC in the same time; then complete the parallelogram ABDC, and by the compounded motion the body will be found in place D at the end of the time; and the curved line AED which the body will describe will be a parabola which the straight line AB touches at A and whose ordinate BD is as AB^2.

What has been demonstrated concerning the times of oscillating pendulums depends on the same first two laws and first two corollaries, and this is supported by daily experience with clocks. From the same laws and corollaries and law 3, Sir Christopher Wren, Dr. John Wallis, and Mr. Christiaan Huygens, easily the foremost geometers of the previous generation, independently found the rules of the collisions and reflections of hard bodies, and communicated them to the Royal Society at nearly the same time, entirely agreeing with one another (as to these rules); and Wallis was indeed the first to publish what had been found, followed by Wren and Huygens. But Wren additionally proved the truth of these rules before the Royal Society by means of an experiment with pendulums, which the eminent Mariotte soon after thought worthy to be made the subject of a whole book.[8]

However, if this experiment is to agree precisely with the theories, account must be taken of both the resistance of the air and the elastic force of the colliding bodies. Let the spherical bodies A and B be suspended from centers C and D by parallel and equal cords AC and BD.

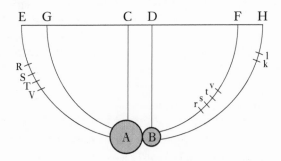

With these centers and with those distances as radii describe semicircles EAF and GBH bisected by radii CA and DB. Take away body B, and let

---

[8] See "A Summary Account of the General Laws of Motion by Dr. John Wallis, and Dr. Christopher Wren," *Philosophical Transactions* 3 (1668): 864–8, and "A Summary Account of the Laws of Motion, Communicated by Mr. Christian Hugens in a Letter to the R. Society," *Philosophical Transactions* 4 (1669): 925–8. Edmé Mariotte wrote *Traité de la Percussion, ou Chocq des Corps dans lequel les Principales Regles du Mouvement* (Paris, 1673), which went into several editions.

body A be brought to any point R of the arc EAF and be let go from there, and let it return after one oscillation to point V. RV is the retardation arising from the resistance of the air. Let ST be a fourth of RV and be located in the middle so that RS and TV are equal and RS is to ST as 3 to 2. Then ST will closely approximate the retardation in the descent from S to A. Restore body B to its original place. Let body A fall from point S, and its velocity at the place of reflection A, without sensible error, will be as great as if it had fallen in a vacuum from place T. Therefore let this velocity be represented by the chord of the arc TA. For it is a proposition very well known to geometers that the velocity of a pendulum in its lowest point is as the chord of the arc that it has described in falling. After reflection let body A arrive at place s, and body B at place k. Take away body B and find place v such that if body A is let go from this place and after one oscillation returns to place r, st will be a fourth of rv and be located in the middle, so that rs and tv are equal; and let the chord of the arc tA represent the velocity that body A had in place A immediately after reflection. For t will be that true and correct place to which body A must have ascended if there had been no resistance of the air. By a similar method the place k, to which body B ascends, will have to be corrected, and the place l, to which that body must have ascended in a vacuum, will have to be found. In this manner it is possible to make all our experiments, just as if we were in a vacuum. Finally body A will have to be multiplied (so to speak) by the chord of the arc TA, which represents its velocity, in order to get its motion in place A immediately before reflection, and then by the chord of the arc tA in order to get its motion in place A immediately after reflection. And thus body B will have to be multiplied by the chord of the arc Bl in order to get its motion immediately after reflection. And by a similar method, when two bodies are let go simultaneously from different places, the motions of both will have to be found before as well as after reflection, and then finally the motions will have to be compared with each other in order to determine the effects of the reflection.

On making a test in this way with ten-foot pendulums, using unequal as well as equal bodies, and making the bodies come together from very large distances apart, say of eight or twelve or sixteen feet, I always found – within an error of less than three inches in the measurements – that when the bodies met each other directly, the changes of motions made in the bodies in opposite directions were equal, and consequently that the action and reaction were always equal. For example, if body A collided with body B, which was at rest, with nine parts of motion and, losing seven parts, proceeded after reflection with two, body B rebounded with those seven parts. If the bodies met head-on, A with twelve parts of motion and B with six, and A rebounded with two, B rebounded with eight, fourteen parts being subtracted from each. Subtract twelve parts from the motion of A and nothing will remain; subtract another two parts, and a motion of two parts in the opposite direction will be produced; and so, subtracting fourteen parts from the six parts of the motion of body B, eight parts will be produced in the opposite direction. But if the bodies moved in the same direction, A more quickly with fourteen parts and B more slowly with five parts, and after reflection A moved with five parts, then B moved with fourteen, nine parts having been transferred from A to B. And so in all other cases. As a result of the meeting and collision of bodies, the quantity of motion – determined by adding the motions in the same direction and subtracting the motions in opposite directions – was never changed. I would attribute the error of an inch or two in the measurements to the difficulty of doing everything with sufficient accuracy. It was difficult both to release the pendulums simultaneously in such a way that the bodies would impinge upon each other in the lowest place AB, and to note the places s and k to which the bodies ascended after colliding. But also, with respect to the pendulous bodies themselves, errors were introduced by the unequal density of the parts and by irregularities of texture arising from other causes.

Further, lest anyone object that the rule which this experiment was designed to prove presupposes that bodies are either absolutely hard or at least perfectly elastic and thus of a kind which do not occur naturally, I add that the experiments just described work equally well with soft bodies and with hard ones, since surely they do not in any way depend on the condition of hardness. For if this rule is to be tested in bodies that are not perfectly hard, it will only be necessary to decrease the reflection in a fixed proportion to the quantity of elastic force. In the theory of Wren and Huygens, absolutely hard bodies rebound from each other with the velocity with which they have collided. This will be affirmed with more certainty of perfectly elastic bodies. In imperfectly elastic bodies the velocity of rebounding must be decreased together with the elastic force, because that force (except when the parts of the bodies are damaged as a result of collision, or experience some sort of extension such as would be caused by a hammer blow) is fixed and determinate (as far as I can tell) and makes the bodies rebound from each other with a relative velocity that is in a given ratio to the relative velocity with which they collide. I have tested this as follows with tightly wound balls of wool strongly compressed. First, releasing the pendulums and measuring their reflection, I found the quantity of their elastic force; then from this force I determined what the reflections would be in other cases of their collision, and the experiments which were made agreed with the computations. The balls always rebounded from each other with a relative velocity that was to the relative velocity of their colliding as 5 to 9, more or less. Steel balls rebounded with nearly the same velocity and cork balls with a slightly smaller velocity, while with glass balls the proportion was roughly 15 to 16. And in this manner the third law of motion – insofar as it relates to impacts and reflections – is proved by this theory, which plainly agrees with experiments.

I demonstrate the third law of motion for attractions briefly as follows.[9] Suppose that between any two bodies A and B that attract each other any obstacle is interposed so as to impede their coming together. If one body A is more attracted toward the other body B than that other body B is attracted toward the first body A, then the obstacle will be more strongly pressed by body A than by body B and accordingly will not remain in equilibrium. The stronger pressure will prevail and will make the system of the two bodies and the obstacle move straight forward in the direction from A toward B and, in empty space, go on indefinitely with a motion that is always accelerated, which is absurd and contrary to the first law of motion. For according to the first law, the system will have to persevere in its state of resting or of moving uniformly straight forward, and accordingly the bodies will urge the obstacle equally and on that account will be equally attracted to each other. I have tested this with a lodestone and iron. If these are placed in separate vessels that touch each other and float side by side in still water, neither one will drive the other forward, but because of the equality of the attraction in both directions they will sustain their mutual endeavors toward each other, and at last, having attained equilibrium, they will be at rest.

In the same way gravity is mutual between the earth and its parts. Let the earth FI be cut by any plane EG into two parts EGF and EGI; then their weights toward each other will be equal. For if the greater part EGI

---

[9] Cf. the discussion in Newton's letter to Cotes, in this volume (pp. 120–2).

is cut into two parts EGKH and HKI by another plane HK parallel to the first plane EG, in such a way that HKI is equal to the part EFG that has been cut off earlier, it is manifest that the middle part EGKH will not preponderate toward either of the outer parts but will, so to speak, be suspended in equilibrium between both and will be at rest. Moreover, the outer part HKI will press upon the middle part with all its weight and will urge it toward the other outer part EGF, and therefore the force by which EGI, the sum of the parts HKI and EGKH, tends toward the third part EGF is equal to the weight of the part HKI, that is, equal to the weight of the third part EGF. And therefore the weights of the two parts EGI and EGF toward each other are equal, as I set out to demonstrate. And if these weights were not equal, the whole earth, floating in an aether free of resistance, would yield to the greater weight and in receding from it would go off indefinitely.

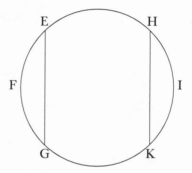

As bodies are equipollent in collisions and reflections if their velocities are inversely as their inherent forces [i.e. forces of inertia], so in the motions of machines those agents [i.e. acting bodies] whose velocities (reckoned in the direction of their forces) are inversely as their inherent forces are equipollent and sustain one another by their contrary endeavors. Thus weights are equipollent in moving the arms of a balance if during oscillation of the balance they are inversely as their velocities upward and downward; that is, weights which move straight up and down are equipollent if they are inversely as the distances between the axis of the balance and the points from which they are suspended; but if such weights are interfered with by oblique planes or other obstacles that are introduced and thus ascend or descend obliquely, they are equipollent if they are inversely as the ascents and descents insofar as these are reckoned with respect to a perpendicular, and this is so because the direction of gravity is downward. Similarly, in a pulley or combination of pulleys, the weight will be sustained by the force of the hand pulling the rope vertically, which is to the weight (ascending either straight up or obliquely) as the velocity of the perpendicular ascent to the velocity of the hand pulling the rope. In clocks and similar devices, which are constructed out of engaged gears, the contrary forces that promote and hinder the motion of the gears will sustain each other if they are inversely as the velocities of the parts of the gears upon which they are impressed. The force of a screw to press a body is to the force of a hand turning the handle as the circular velocity of the handle, in the part where it is urged by the hand, is to the progressive velocity of the screw toward the pressed body. The forces by which a wedge presses the two parts of the wood that it splits are to the force of the hammer upon the wedge as the progress of the wedge (in the direction of the force impressed upon it by the hammer) is to the velocity with which the parts of the wood yield to the wedge along lines perpendicular to the faces of the wedge. And the case is the same for all machines.

The effectiveness and usefulness of all machines or devices consist wholly in our being able to increase the force by decreasing the velocity, and vice versa; in this way the problem is solved in the case of any working machine or device: "To move a given weight by a given force" or to overcome any other given resistance by a given force. For if machines are constructed in such a way that the velocities of the agent [or acting body] and the resistant [or resisting body] are inversely as the forces, the agent will sustain the resistance and, if there is a greater disparity of velocities, will overcome that resistance. Of course the disparity of the velocities may be so great that it can also overcome all the resistance which generally arises from the friction of contiguous bodies sliding over one another, from the cohesion of continuous bodies that are to be separated from one another, or from the weights of bodies to be raised; and if all this resistance is overcome, the remaining force will produce an acceleration of motion proportional to itself, partly in the parts of the machine, partly in the resisting body.

But my purpose here is not to write a treatise on mechanics. By these examples I wished only to show the wide range and the certainty of the third law of motion. For if the action of an agent is reckoned by its force and velocity jointly, and if, similarly, the reaction of a resistant is reckoned jointly by the velocities of its individual parts and the forces of resistance arising from their friction, cohesion, weight, and acceleration, the action and reaction will always be equal to each other in all examples of using devices or machines. And to the extent to which the action is propagated through the machine and ultimately impressed upon each resisting body, its ultimate direction will always be opposite to the direction of the reaction.

Book One: The Motions of Bodies

Book One: Section 11

Scholium

By these propositions we are directed to the analogy between centripetal forces and the central bodies toward which those forces tend. For it is reasonable that forces directed toward bodies depend on the nature and the quantity of matter of such bodies, as happens in the case of magnetic bodies. And whenever cases of this sort occur, the attractions of the bodies must be reckoned by assigning proper forces to their individual particles and then taking the sums of these forces.

I use the word 'attraction' here in a general sense for any endeavor whatever of bodies to approach one another, whether that endeavor occurs as a result of the action of the bodies either drawn toward one another or acting on one another by means of spirits emitted or whether it arises from the action of aether or of air or of any medium whatsoever – whether corporeal or incorporeal – in any way impelling toward one another the bodies floating therein. I use the word 'impulse' in the same general sense, considering in this treatise not the species of forces and their physical qualities but their quantities and mathematical proportions, as I have explained in the definitions.

Mathematics requires an investigation of those quantities of forces and their proportions that follow from any conditions that may be supposed. Then, coming down to physics, these proportions must be compared with the phenomena, so that it may be found out which conditions [or laws] of forces apply to each kind of attracting bodies. And then, finally, it will be possible to argue more securely concerning the physical species, physical causes, and physical proportions of these forces. Let us see, therefore, what the forces are by which spherical bodies, consisting of particles that attract in the way already set forth, must act upon one another, and what sorts of motions result from such forces.

Book Three: The System of the World

Rules for the Study of Natural Philosophy

Rule 1

No more causes of natural things should be admitted than are both true and sufficient to explain their phenomena.

As the philosophers say: Nature does nothing in vain, and more causes are in vain when fewer suffice. For nature is simple and does not indulge in the luxury of superfluous causes.

Rule 2

Therefore, the causes assigned to natural effects of the same kind must be, so far as possible, the same.

Examples are the cause of respiration in man and beast, or of the falling of stones in Europe and America, or of the light of a kitchen fire and the sun, or of the reflection of light on our earth and the planets.

Rule 3

Those qualities of bodies that cannot be intended and remitted [i.e. increased and diminished] and that belong to all bodies on which experiments can be made should be taken as qualities of all bodies universally.

For the qualities of bodies can be known only through experiments; and therefore qualities that square with experiments universally are to be regarded as universal qualities; and qualities that cannot be diminished cannot be taken away from bodies. Certainly idle fancies ought not to be fabricated recklessly against the evidence of experiments, nor should we depart from the analogy of nature, since nature is always simple and ever consonant with itself. The extension of bodies is known to us only through our senses, and yet there are bodies beyond the range of these senses; but because extension is found in all sensible bodies, it is ascribed to all bodies universally. We know by experience that some bodies are hard. Moreover, because the hardness of the whole arises from the hardness of its parts, we justly infer from this not only the hardness of the undivided particles of bodies that are accessible to our senses, but also of all other bodies. That all bodies are impenetrable we gather not by reason but by our senses. We find those bodies that we handle to be impenetrable, and hence we conclude that impenetrability is a property of all bodies universally. That all bodies are movable and persevere in motion or in rest by means of certain forces (which we call forces of inertia) we infer from finding these properties in the bodies that we have seen. The extension, hardness, impenetrability, mobility, and force of inertia of the whole arise from the extension, hardness, impenetrability, mobility, and force of inertia of each of the parts; and thus we conclude that every one of the least parts of all bodies is extended, hard, impenetrable, movable, and endowed with a force of inertia. And this is the foundation of all natural philosophy. Further, from phenomena we know that the divided, contiguous parts of bodies can be separated from one another, and from mathematics it is certain that the undivided parts can be distinguished into smaller parts by our reason. But it is uncertain whether those parts which have been distinguished in this way and not yet divided can actually be divided and separated from one another by the forces of nature. But if it were established by even a single experiment that in the breaking of a hard and solid body, any undivided particle underwent division, we should conclude by the force of this third rule not only that divided parts are separable but also that undivided parts can be divided indefinitely.

Finally, if it is universally established by experiments and astronomical observations that all bodies on or near the earth gravitate [literally, are heavy] toward the earth, and do so in proportion to the quantity of matter in each body, and that the moon gravitates [is heavy] toward the earth in proportion to the quantity of its matter, and that our sea in turn gravitates [is heavy] toward the moon, and that all planets gravitate [are heavy] toward one another, and that there is a similar gravity [heaviness] of comets toward the sun, it will have to be concluded by this third rule that all bodies gravitate toward one another. Indeed, the argument from phenomena will be even stronger for universal gravity than for the impenetrability of bodies, for which, of course, we have not a single experiment, and not even an observation, in the case of the heavenly bodies. Yet I am by no means affirming that gravity is essential to bodies. By inherent force I mean only the force of inertia. This is immutable. Gravity is diminished as bodies recede from the earth.

Rule 4

In experimental philosophy, propositions gathered from phenomena by induction should be considered either exactly or very nearly true notwithstanding any contrary hypotheses, until yet other phenomena make such propositions either more exact or liable to exceptions.

This rule should be followed so that arguments based on induction may not be nullified by hypotheses.

General Scholium

The hypothesis of vortices is beset with many difficulties. If, by a radius drawn to the sun, each and every planet is to describe areas proportional to the time, the periodic times of the parts of the vortex must be as the squares of the distances from the sun. If the periodic times of the planets are to be as the 3/2 powers of the distances from the sun, the periodic times of the parts of the vortex must be as the 3/2 powers of the distances. If the smaller vortices revolving about Saturn, Jupiter, and the other planets are to be preserved and are to float without agitation in the vortex of the sun, the periodic times of the parts of the solar vortex must be the same. The axial revolutions [i.e. rotations] of the sun and planets, which would have to agree with the motions of their vortices, differ from all these proportions. The motions of comets are extremely regular, observe the same laws as the motions of planets, and cannot be explained by vortices. Comets go with very eccentric motions into all parts of the heavens, which cannot happen unless vortices are eliminated.[10]

The only resistance which projectiles encounter in our air is from the air. With the air removed, as it is in Boyle's vacuum, resistance ceases, since a tenuous feather and solid gold fall with equal velocity in such a vacuum. And the case is the same for the celestial spaces, which are above the atmosphere of the earth. All bodies must move very freely in these spaces, and therefore planets and comets must revolve continually in orbits given in kind and in position, according to the laws set forth

[10] Cf. again Newton's 1693 letter to Leibniz, in this volume.

above. They will indeed persevere in their orbits by the laws of gravity, but they certainly could not originally have acquired the regular position of the orbits by these laws.

The six primary planets revolve about the sun in circles concentric with the sun, with the same direction of motion, and very nearly in the same plane. Ten moons revolve about the earth, Jupiter, and Saturn in concentric circles, with the same direction of motion, very nearly in the planes of the orbits of the planets. And all these regular motions do not have their origin in mechanical causes, since comets go freely in very eccentric orbits and into all parts of the heavens. And with this kind of motion the comets pass very swiftly and very easily through the orbits of the planets; and in their aphelia, where they are slower and spend a longer time, they are at the greatest possible distance from one another, so as to attract one another as little as possible.

This most elegant system of the sun, planets, and comets could not have arisen without the design and dominion of an intelligent and powerful being. And if the fixed stars are the centers of similar systems, they will all be constructed according to a similar design and subject to the dominion of *One*, especially since the light of the fixed stars is of the same nature as the light of the sun, and all the systems send light into all the others. And so that the systems of the fixed stars will not fall upon one another as a result of their gravity, he has placed them at immense distances from one another.

He rules all things, not as the world soul but as the lord of all. And because of his dominion he is called Lord God *Pantokrator* [i.e. universal ruler]. For 'god' is a relative word and has reference to servants, and godhood is the lordship of God, not over his own body as is supposed by those for whom God is the world soul, but over servants. The supreme God is an eternal, infinite, and absolutely perfect being; but a being, however perfect, without dominion is not the Lord God. For we do say my God, your God, the God of Israel, the God of Gods, and Lord of Lords, but we do not say my eternal one, your eternal one, the eternal one of Israel, the eternal one of the gods; we do not say my infinite one, or my perfect one. These designations [i.e. eternal, infinite, perfect] do not have reference to servants. The word 'god' is used far and wide to mean "lord," but every lord is not a god. The lordship of a spiritual being constitutes a god, a true lordship constitutes a true god, a supreme lordship a supreme god, an imaginary lordship an imaginary god. And from true lordship it follows that the true God is living, intelligent, and powerful; from the other perfections, that he is supreme, or supremely perfect. He is eternal and infinite, omnipotent and omniscient, that is, he endures from eternity to eternity, and he is present from infinity to infinity; he rules all things, and he knows all things that happen or can happen. He is not eternity and infinity, but eternal and infinite; he is not duration and space, but he endures and is present. He endures always and is present everywhere, and by existing always and everywhere he constitutes duration and space. Since each and every particle of space is *always*, and each and every indivisible moment of duration is *everywhere*, certainly the maker and lord of all things will not be *never* or *nowhere*.

Every sentient soul, at different times and in different organs of senses and motions, is the same indivisible person. There are parts that are successive in duration and coexistent in space, but neither of these exist in the person of man or in his thinking principle, and much less in the thinking substance of God. Every man, insofar as he is a thing that has senses, is one and the same man throughout his lifetime in each and every organ of his senses. God is one and the same God always and everywhere. He is omnipresent not only *virtually* but also *substantially*; for action requires substance. In him all things are contained and move, but he does not act on them nor they on him.

It is agreed that the supreme God necessarily exists, and by the same necessity he is *always* and *everywhere*. It follows that all of him is like himself: he is all eye, all ear, all brain, all arm, all force of sensing, of understanding, and of acting, but in a way not at all human, in a way not at all corporeal, in a way utterly unknown to us. As a blind man has no idea of colors, so we have no idea of the ways in which the most wise God senses and understands all things. He totally lacks any body and corporeal shape, and so he cannot be seen or heard or touched, nor ought he to be worshiped in the form of something corporeal. We have ideas of his attributes, but we certainly do not know what is the substance of any thing. We see only the shapes and colors of bodies, we hear only their sounds, we touch only their external surfaces, we smell only their odors, and we taste their flavors. But there is no direct sense and there are no indirect reflected actions by which we know innermost substances; much less do we have an idea of the substance of God. We know him only by his properties and attributes and by the wisest and best construction of things and their final causes, and we admire him because of his perfections; but we venerate and worship him because of his dominion. For we worship him as servants, and a god without dominion, providence, and final causes is nothing other than fate and nature. No variation of things arises from blind metaphysical necessity, which must be the same always and everywhere. All the diversity of created things, each in its place and time, could only have arisen from the ideas and the will of a necessarily existing being. But God is said allegorically to see, hear, speak, laugh, love, hate, desire, give, receive, be angry, fight, build, form, construct. For all discourse about God is derived through a certain similitude from things human, which while not perfect is nevertheless a similitude of some kind. This concludes the discussion of God, and to treat of God from phenomena is certainly a part of natural philosophy.

Thus far I have explained the phenomena of the heavens and of our sea by the force of gravity, but I have not yet assigned a cause to gravity. Indeed, this force arises from some cause that penetrates as far as the centers of the sun and planets without any diminution of its power to act, and that acts not in proportion to the quantity of the *surfaces* of the particles on which it acts (as mechanical causes are wont to do) but in proportion to the quantity of *solid* matter, and whose action is extended everywhere to immense distances, always decreasing as the squares of the distances. Gravity toward the sun is compounded of the gravities toward the individual particles of the sun, and at increasing distances from the sun decreases exactly as the squares of the distances as far out as the orbit of Saturn, as is manifest from the fact that the aphelia of the planets are at rest, and even as far as the farthest aphelia of the comets, provided that those aphelia are at rest. I have not as yet been able to deduce from phenomena the reason for these properties of gravity, and I do not feign hypotheses. For whatever is not deduced from the phenomena must be called a hypothesis; and hypotheses, whether metaphysical or physical, or based on occult qualities, or mechanical, have no place in experimental philosophy. In this experimental philosophy, propositions are deduced from the phenomena and are made general by induction. The impenetrability, mobility, and impetus of bodies, and the laws of motion and the law of gravity have been found by this method. And it is enough that gravity really exists and acts according to the laws that we have set forth and is sufficient to explain all the motions of the heavenly bodies and of our sea.

A few things could now be added concerning a certain very subtle
spirit pervading gross bodies and lying hidden in them; by its force and
actions, the particles of bodies attract one another at very small distances
and cohere when they become contiguous; and electrical [i.e. electrified]
bodies act at greater distances, repelling as well as attracting neighboring
corpuscles; and light is emitted, reflected, refracted, inflected, and heats
bodies; and all sensation is excited, and the limbs of animals move at command of the will, namely, by the vibrations of this spirit being propagated
through the solid fibers of the nerves from the external organs of the
senses to the brain and from the brain into the muscles. But these things
cannot be explained in a few words; furthermore, there is not a sufficient
number of experiments to determine and demonstrate accurately the laws
governing the actions of this spirit.

IV

Correspondence with Richard Bentley [1692–3]

LETTER ONE
Cambridge, 10 December 1692

To the Reverend Dr Richard Bentley, at the Bishop of Worcester's House in Parkstreet, Westminster.

SIR,

W H E N I wrote my treatise about our system,[1] I had an eye upon such principles as might work with considering men, for the belief of a deity, and nothing can rejoice me more than to find it useful for that purpose. But if I have done the public any service this way, it is due to nothing but industry and patient thought.

As to your first query, it seems to me that if the matter of our sun and planets, and all the matter of the universe, were evenly scattered throughout all the heavens, and every particle had an innate gravity towards all the rest, and the whole space, throughout which this matter was scattered, was but finite; the matter on the outside of this space would by its gravity tend towards all the matter on the inside, and by consequence fall down into the middle of the whole space, and there compose one great spherical mass. But if the matter was evenly dispersed throughout an infinite space, it would never convene into one mass, but some of it would convene into one mass and some into another, so as to make an infinite number of great masses, scattered at great distances from one to another throughout all that infinite space. And thus might the sun and fixed stars be formed, supposing the matter were of a lucid nature. But how the matter should

---

[1] That is, the *Principia*.

94

divide itself into two sorts, and that part of it, which is fit to compose a shining body, should fall down into one mass and make a sun, and the rest, which is fit to compose an opaque body, should coalesce, not into one great body, like the shining matter, but into many little ones or if the sun at first were an opaque body like the planets, or the planets lucid bodies like the sun, how it alone should be changed into a shining body, while all they continue opaque, or all they be changed into opaque ones, while it remains unchanged, I do not think explicable by mere natural causes, but am forced to ascribe it to the counsel and contrivance of a voluntary agent.

The same power, whether natural or supernatural, which placed the sun in the centre of the six primary planets, placed Saturn in the centre of the orbits of its five secondary planets, and Jupiter in the centre of its four secondary planets, and the earth in the centre of the moon's orbit; and therefore had this cause been a blind one, without contrivance or design, the sun would have been a body of the same kind with Saturn, Jupiter, and the earth, that is, without light and heat. Why there is one body in our system qualified to give light and heat to all the rest, I know no reason, but because the author of the system thought it convenient; and why there is but one body of this kind I know no reason, but because one was sufficient to warm and enlighten all the rest. For the Cartesian hypothesis of suns losing their light, and then turning into comets, and comets into planets, can have no place in my system, and is plainly erroneous; because it is certain that as often as they appear to us, they descend into the system of our planets, lower than the orbit of Jupiter, and sometimes lower than the orbits of Venus and Mercury, and yet never stay here, but always return from the sun with the same degrees of motion by which they approached it.

To your second query, I answer, that the motions which the planets now have could not spring from any natural cause alone, but were impressed by an intelligent agent. For since comets descend into the region of our planets, and here move all manner of ways, going some times the same way with the planets, sometimes the contrary way, and sometimes in cross ways, in planes inclined to the plane of the ecliptic, and at all kinds of angles, it is plain that there is no natural cause which could determine all the planets, both primary and secondary, to move the same way and in the same plane, without any considerable variation. This must have been the effect of counsel. Nor is there any natural cause which could give the planets those just degrees of velocity, in proportion to their distances from the sun, and other central bodies, which were requisite to make them move in such concentric orbits about those bodies. Had the planets been as swift as comets, in proportion to their distances from the sun (as they would have been, had their motion been caused by their gravity, whereby the matter, at the first formation of the planets, might fall from the remote regions towards the sun), they would not move in concentric orbits, but in such eccentric ones as the comets move in. Were all the planets as swift as Mercury, or as slow as Saturn or its satellites; or were their several velocities otherwise much greater or less than they are, as they might have been had they arose from any other cause than their gravities; or had the distances from the centres about which they move been greater or less than they are with the same velocities; or had the quantity of matter in the sun, or in Saturn, Jupiter, and the earth, and by consequence their gravitating power, been greater or less than it is; the primary planets could not have revolved about the sun, nor the secondary ones about Saturn, Jupiter, and the earth, in concentric circles as they do, but would have moved in hyperbolas, or parabolas, or in ellipses very eccentric. To make this system, therefore, with all its motions, required a cause which understood, and compared together, the quantities of matter in the several bodies of the sun and planets, and the gravitating powers resulting from thence; the several distances of the primary planets from the sun, and of the secondary ones from Saturn, Jupiter, and the earth; and the velocities with which these planets could revolve about those quantities of matter in the central bodies; and to compare and adjust all these things together, in so great a variety of bodies, argues that cause to be not blind and fortuitous, but very well skilled in mechanics and geometry.

To your third query, I answer, that it may be represented that the sun may, by heating those planets most which are nearest to it, cause them to be better concocted, and more condensed by concoction. But when I consider that our earth is much more heated in its bowels below the upper crust by subterraneous fermentations of mineral bodies than by the sun, I see not why the interior parts of Jupiter and Saturn might not be as much heated, concocted, and coagulated by those fermentations as our earth is and therefore this various density should have some other cause than the various distances of the planets from the sun. And I am confirmed in this opinion by considering that the planets Jupiter and Saturn, as they are rarer than the rest, so they are vastly greater, and contain a far greater quantity of matter, and have many satellites about them; which qualifications surely arose not from their being placed at so great a distance from the sun, but were rather the cause why the creator placed them at that great distance. For by their gravitating powers they disturb one another's motions very sensibly, as I find by some late observations of Mr Flamsteed,[2] and had they been placed much nearer to the sun and to one another, they would by the same powers have caused a considerable disturbance in the whole system.

To your fourth query, I answer, that in the hypothesis of vortices, the inclination of the axis of the earth might, in my opinion, be ascribed to the situation of the earth's vortex before it was absorbed by the neighbouring vortices, and the earth turned from a sun to a comet; but this inclination ought to decrease constantly in compliance with the motion of the earth's vortex, whose axis is much less inclined to the ecliptic, as appears by the motion of the moon carried about therein. If the sun by its rays could carry about the planets, yet I do not see how it could thereby effect their diurnal motions.

Lastly, I see nothing extraordinary in the inclination of the earth's axis for proving a deity, unless you will urge it as a contrivance for winter and summer, and for making the earth habitable towards the poles; and that the diurnal rotations of the sun and planets, as they could hardly arise from any cause purely mechanical, so by being determined all the same way with the annual and menstrual motions, they seem to make up that harmony in the system, which, as I explained above, was the effect of choice rather than chance.

There is yet another argument for a deity, which I take to be a very strong one, but till the principles on which it is grounded are better received, I think it more advisable to let it sleep.

I am,
Your most humble Servant to command,
Is. Newton

---

[2] John Flamsteed was an astronomer working in Greenwich whose observational data proved important for Newton's work in the *Principia*, and with whom Newton corresponded (and fought) frequently.

LETTER TWO

Cambridge, 17 January 1692/3

For Mr. BENTLEY, at the Palace at Worcester.

SIR,

I agree with you, that if matter evenly diffused through a finite space, not spherical, should fall into a solid mass, this mass would affect the figure of the whole space, provided it were not soft, like the old chaos, but so hard and solid from the beginning that the weight of its protuberant parts could not make it yield to their pressure. Yet by earthquakes loosening the parts of this solid, the protuberances might sometimes sink a little by their weight, and thereby the mass might, by degrees, approach a spherical figure.

The reason why matter evenly scattered through a finite space would convene in the midst, you conceive the same with me; but that there should be a central particle, so accurately placed in the middle, as to be always equally attracted on all sides, and thereby continue without motion, seems to me a supposition fully as hard as to make the sharpest needle land upright on its point upon a looking glass. For if the very mathematical centre of the central particle be not accurately in the very mathematical centre of the attractive power of the whole mass, the particle will not be attracted equally on all sides. And much harder it is to suppose that all the particles in an infinite space should be so accurately poised one among another, as to stand still in a perfect equilibrium. For I reckon this as hard as to make not one needle only, but an infinite number of them (so many as there are particles in an infinite space) stand accurately poised upon their points. Yet I grant it possible, at least by a divine power; and if they were once to be placed, I agree with you that they would continue in that posture without motion forever, unless put into new motion by the same power. When therefore I said that matter evenly spread through all space would convene by its gravity into one or more great masses, I understand it of matter not resting in an accurate poise.

But you argue, in the next paragraph of your letter, that every particle of matter in an infinite space has an infinite quantity of matter on all sides, and by consequence an infinite attraction every way, and therefore must rest in equilibrium, because all infinites are equal. Yet you suspect a paralogism[3] in this argument; and I conceive the paralogism lies in the

---

[3] An error in reasoning.

position, that all infinites are equal. The generality of mankind consider infinites no other ways than indefinitely; and in this sense, they say all infinites are equal; though they would speak more truly if they should say, they are neither equal nor unequal, nor have any certain difference or proportion one to another. In this sense, therefore, no conclusions can be drawn from them about the equality, proportions, or differences of things, and they that attempt to do it usually fall into paralogisms. So when men argue against the infinite divisibility of magnitude, by saying that if an inch may be divided into an infinite number of parts, the sum of those parts will be an inch; and if a foot may be divided into an infinite number of parts, the sum of those parts must be a foot, and therefore since all infinites are equal, those sums must be equal, that is, an inch equal to a foot.

The falseness of the conclusion shows an error in the premises, and the error lies in the position, that all infinites are equal. There is therefore another way of considering infinites used by mathematicians, and that is, under certain definite restrictions and limitations, whereby infinites are determined to have certain differences or proportions to one another. Thus Dr. Wallis considers them in his *Arithmetica Infinitorium*,[4] where by the various proportions of infinite sums, he gathers the various proportions of infinite magnitudes: which way of arguing is generally allowed by mathematicians, and yet would not be good were all infinites equal. According to the same way of considering infinites, a mathematician would tell you, that though there be an infinite number of infinitely little parts in an inch, yet there is twelve times that number of such parts in a foot, that is, the infinite number of those parts in a foot is not equal to, but twelve times bigger than, the infinite number of them in an inch. And so a mathematician will tell you, that if a body stood in equilibrium between any two equal and contrary attracting infinite forces; and if to either of these forces you add any new finite attracting force, that new force, how little whatsoever, will destroy their equilibrium, and put the body into the same motion into which it would put it were those two contrary equal forces but finite, or even none at all; so that in this case the two equal infinites by the addition of a finite to either of them, become unequal in our ways of reckoning. And after these ways we must reckon if from the considerations of infinites we would always draw true conclusions.

---

[4] Newton refers here to John Wallis, *The Arithmetic of Infinites*, or *Arithmetica Infinitorum, sive Nova Methodus Inquirendi in Curvilineorum Quadraturam* (Oxford, 1656).

To the last part of your letter, I answer, first, that if the earth (without the moon) were placed anywhere with its centre in the *Orbis Magnus* [the earth's solar orbit], and stood still there without any gravitation or projection, and there at once were infused into it both a gravitating energy towards the sun and a transverse impulse of a just quantity, moving it directly in a tangent to the *Orbis Magnus*, the compounds of this attraction and projection would, according to my notion, cause a circular revolution of the earth about the sun. But the transverse impulse must be a just quantity, for if it be too big or too little, it will cause the earth to move in some other line. Secondly, I do not know any power in nature which could cause this transverse motion without the divine arm. Blondel tells us somewhere in his book of bombs,[5] that Plato affirms that the motion of the planets is such, as if they had all of them been created by God in some region very remote from our system, and let fall from thence towards the sun, and so soon as they arrived at their several orbits, their motion of falling turned aside into a transverse one. And this is true, supposing the gravitating power of the sun was double at that moment of time in which they all arrive at their several orbits; but then the divine power is here required in a double respect, namely, to turn the descending motions of the falling planets into a side motion, and at the same time to double the attractive power of the sun. So then gravity may put the planets into motion, but without the divine power it could never put them into such a circulating motion as they have about the sun; and therefore, for this, as well as other reasons, I am compelled to ascribe the frame of this system to an intelligent agent.

You sometimes speak of gravity as essential and inherent to matter. Pray do not ascribe that notion to me; for the cause of gravity is what I do not pretend to know, and therefore would take more time to consider of it. I fear what I have said of infinites, will seem obscure to you; but it is enough if you understand, that infinites when considered absolutely without any restriction or limitation, are neither equal nor unequal, nor have any certain proportion one to another, and therefore the principle that all infinites are equal, is a precarious one.

Sir, I am,
Your most humble Servant,
Is. Newton

---

5 The reference is to François Blondel, *L'Art de Jetter les Bombes* (Paris, 1683).

To Mr BENTLEY, at the Palace at Worcester.

SIR,

The hypothesis of deriving the frame of the world by mechanical principles from matter evenly spread through the heavens, being inconsistent with my system, I had considered it very little before your letters put me upon it, and therefore trouble you with a line or two more about it, if this comes not too late for your use.

In my former [letter] I represented that the diurnal rotations of the planets could not be derived from gravity, but required a divine arm to impress them. And though gravity might give the planets a motion of descent towards the sun, either directly or with some little obliquity, yet the transverse motions by which they revolve in their several orbits required the divine arm to impress them according to the tangents of their orbits. I would now add, that the hypothesis of matter's being at first evenly spread through the heavens is, in my opinion, inconsistent with the hypothesis of innate gravity, without a supernatural power to reconcile them, and therefore it infers [i.e. implies] a deity. For if there be innate gravity, it is impossible now for the matter of the earth and all the planets and stars to fly up from them, and become evenly spread throughout all the heavens, without a supernatural power, and certainly that which can never be hereafter without a supernatural power, could never be heretofore without the same powers. You queried, whether matter evenly spread throughout a finite space, of some other figure than spherical, would not in falling down towards a central body cause that body to be of the same figure with the whole space, and I answered, yes. But in my answer it is to be supposed that the matter descends directly downwards to that body, and that that body has no diurnal rotation.

This, Sir, is all I would add to my former letters.

I am, Your most humble Servant,
Is. Newton

For Mr BENTLEY, at the Palace at Worcester.

SIR,

Because you desire speed, I will answer your letter with what brevity I can. In the six positions you lay down in the beginning of your letter, I agree with you. Your assuming the *Orbis Magnus* [the earth's solar orbit] 7,000 diameters of the earth wide, implies the sun's horizontal parallax to be half a minute. Flamsteed and Cassini[6] have of late observed it to be about 10″, and thus the *Orbis Magnus* must be 21,000 or in a rounder number 20,000 diameters of the earth wide. Either computation I think will do well, and I think it not worthwhile to alter your numbers.

In the next part of your letter you lay down four other positions, founded upon the six first. The first of these four seems very evident, supposing you take attraction so generally as by it to understand any force by which distant bodies endeavour to come together without mechanical impulse. The second seems not so clear; for it may be said, that there might be other systems of worlds before the present ones, and others before those, and so on to all past eternity, and by consequence that gravity may be coeternal to matter, and have the same effect from all eternity as at present, unless you have somewhere proved that old systems cannot gradually pass into new ones, or that this system had not its original from the exhaling matter of former decaying systems, but from a chaos of matter evenly dispersed throughout all space; for something of this kind, I think, you say was the subject of your sixth sermon; and the growth of new systems out of old ones, without the mediation of a divine power, seems to me apparently absurd.

The last clause of the second position I like very well. It is inconceivable that inanimate brute matter should, without the mediation of something else, which is not material, operate upon and affect other matter without mutual contact, as it must be, if gravitation in the sense of Epicurus, be essential and inherent in it. And this is one reason why I desired you would not ascribe innate gravity to me. That gravity should be innate, inherent, and essential to matter, so that one body may act upon another at a distance through a vacuum without the mediation of anything else, by and through which their action and force may be conveyed from one to another, is to me so great an absurdity, that I believe no man who has in philosophical matters a competent faculty of thinking can ever fall into it.

---

[6] See the note on p. 97 about Flamsteed; Jean-Dominique Cassini presented important astronomical data including, among other things, observations of Jupiter and Saturn.

Gravity must be caused by an agent acing constantly according to certain laws; but whether this agent be material or immaterial, I have left to the consideration of my readers.

Your fourth assertion, that the world could not be formed by innate gravity alone, you confirm by three arguments. But in your first argument you seem to make a *petitio principii*;[7] for whereas many ancient philosophers and others, as well theists as atheists, have all allowed that there may be worlds and parcels of matter innumerable or infinite, you deny this by representing it as absurd as that there should be positively an infinite arithmetical sum or number, which is a contradiction in terms; but you do not prove it as absurd. Neither do you prove that what men mean by an infinite sum or number is a contradiction in nature, for a contradiction in terms implies no more than an impropriety of speech. Those things which men understand by improper and contradictious phrases may be sometimes really in nature without any contradiction at all. A silver inkhorn, a paper lantern, an iron whetstone, [are] absurd phrases, yet the things signified thereby are really in nature. If any man should say that a number and a sum, to speak properly, is that which may be numbered and summed, but things infinite are numberless, or as we usually speak, innumerable and sumless, or insummable, and therefore ought not to be called a number or sum, he will speak properly enough, and your argument against him will, I fear, lose its force. And yet if any man shall take the words number and sum in a larger sense, so as to understand thereby things which in the proper way of speaking are numberless and sumless (as you seem to do when you allow an infinite number of points in a line), I could readily allow him the use of the contradictious phrases of innumerable number, or sumless sum, without inferring from thence any absurdity in the thing he means by those phrases. However, if by this, or any other argument, you have proved the finiteness of the universe, it follows, that all matter would fall down from the outsides, and convene in the middle. Yet the matter in falling might concrete into many round masses, like the bodies of the planets, and these by attracting one another might acquire an obliquity of descent, by means of which they might fall, not upon the great central body, but upon the side of it, and fetch a compass about, and then ascend again by the same steps and degrees of motion and velocity with which they descended before, much after the manner that the comets revolve

[7] A begging of the question at issue.

about the sun; but a circular motion in concentric orbits about the sun they could never acquire by gravity alone.

And though all the matter were divided at first into several systems, and every system by a divine power constituted like ours: yet would the outside systems descend towards the middlemost so that this frame of things could not always subsist without a divine power to conserve it, which is the second argument; and to your third I fully assent.

As for the passage of Plato, there is no common place from whence all the planets being let fall, and descending with uniform and equal gravities (as Galileo supposes), would at their arrival to their several orbits acquire their several velocities, with which they now revolve in them. If we suppose the gravity of all the planets towards the sun to be of such a quantity as it really is, and that the motions of the planets are turned upwards, every planet will ascend to twice its height from the sun. Saturn will ascend till it be twice as high from the sun as it is at present, and no higher; Jupiter will ascend as high again as at present, that is, a little above the orbit of Saturn. Mercury will ascend to twice its present height, that is, to the orbit of Venus; and so of the rest. And then by falling down again from the places to which they ascended, they will arrive again at their several orbits with the same velocities they had at first, and with which they now revolve. But if so soon as their motions by which they revolve are turned upwards, the gravitating power of the sun, by which their ascent is perpetually retarded, be diminished by one half, they will now ascend perpetually, and all of them at all equal distances from the sun will be equally swift. Mercury when it arrives at the orbit of Venus, will be as swift as Venus; and it and Venus, when they arrive at the orbit of the earth, will be as swift as the earth; and so of the rest. If they begin all of them to ascend at once, and ascend in the same line, they will constantly in ascending become nearer and nearer together, and their motions will constantly approach to an equality, and become at length slower than any motion assignable. Suppose therefore that they ascended till they were almost contiguous, and their motions inconsiderably little, and that all their motions were at the same moment of time turned back again, or which comes almost to the same thing, that they were only deprived of their motions, and let fall at that time, they would all at once arrive at their several orbits, each with the velocity it had at first; and if their motions were then turned sideways, and at the same time the gravitating power of the sun doubled, that it might be strong enough to retain them in their orbits, they would revolve in them as before their ascent. But if the gravitating power of the sun was not doubled, they would go away from their orbits into the highest heavens in parabolical lines. These things follow from my *Mathematical Principles of Natural Philosophy*, Book One, Propositions 33, 34, 36, 37.

I thank you very kindly for your designed present, and rest

Your most humble Servant to command,
Is. Newton

V

Correspondence with Leibniz [1693/1712]

LEIBNIZ TO NEWTON

Hanover, 7 March 1692/3

To the celebrated Isaac Newton:
Gottfried Wilhelm Leibniz sends cordial greetings

How great I think the debt owed to you, by our knowledge of mathematics and of all nature, I have acknowledged in public also when occasion offered. You had given an astonishing development to geometry by your series; but when you published your work, the *Principia*, you showed that even what is not subject to the received analysis is an open book to you. I too have tried by the application of convenient symbols, which exhibit differences and sums, to submit that geometry which I call "transcendent" in some sense to analysis, and the attempt did not go badly . . . [.]

But above all I would wish that, perfected in geometrical problems, you would continue, as you have begun, to handle nature in mathematical terms; and in this field you have by yourself with very few companions gained an immense return for your labor. You have made the astonishing discovery that Kepler's ellipses result simply from the conception of attraction or gravitation and passage in a planet. And yet I would incline to believe that all these are caused or regulated by the motion of a fluid medium, on the analogy of gravity and magnetism as we know it here.[1]

---

[1] Leibniz here signals his desire to defend a vortex theory of gravity, the vortex being the "fluid medium" he mentions. His primary response to the theory of gravity outlined in the *Principia*,

Yet this solution would not at all detract from the value and truth of your discovery. I do not doubt that you have weighed what Christiaan Huygens, that other supreme mathematician, has remarked in the appendix to his book about the cause of light and gravity.[2] I would like your opinion in reply: for it is by the friendly collaboration of you eminent specialists in this field that the truth can best be unearthed.

Now, as you also have thrown most light on precisely the science of dioptrics by explaining unexpected phenomena of colors, I would like your opinion about Huygens's explanation of light, assuredly a most brilliant one since the law of sines works out so happily.[3] Huygens indicated to me that you had informed him of some new phenomena of colors. I would like it very much if the system of the so-called fixed colors could be deduced from apparent colors, or else that the method of producing them by refractions could be demonstrated so that some whole surface should display a definite color.

In catalogues of books published in England I several times came across books on mathematics by Newton. But I was in doubt whether they were by you, as I hope, or by another of the same name.[4]

My fellow countryman Heinson[5] on his return assured me of your friendly feelings towards me. But of my veneration for you not only he can testify, but Stepney too, once your fellow resident in the same College, now his Britannic Majesty's ambassador to the Imperial Court, lately to his Serene Highness the Elector of Brandenburg.[6]

I write this rather that you should understand my devotion to you, a devotion that has lost nothing by the silence of so many years,[7] than that with empty, and worse than empty, letters I should interrupt the devoted studies by which you increase the patrimony of mankind. Farewell.

---

the *Tentamen* of 1689, outlines his vortex theory in detail. The *Tentamen* is available in English translation and in a critical edition by Meli, *Equivalence and Priority*.

[2] In 1690, Huygens's *Treatise on Light* and *Discourse on the Cause of Gravity* appeared in one volume in French from a publisher in Leiden; Newton had this edition in his library.

[3] In his *Treatise on Light*, Huygens deduces the laws of reflection and refraction from a principle he introduces in discussing the process of wave propagation.

[4] They were not in fact by Newton, but rather by John Newton (1622–78).

[5] He refers to Johann Theodor Heinson, who had been elected to the Royal Society as a fellow in 1692.

[6] George Stepney was a fellow of Trinity College, Cambridge in 1687.

[7] The last letter was written on 12 July 1677.

NEWTON TO LEIBNIZ
Cambridge, 16 October 1693

To the celebrated Gottfried Wilhelm Leibniz:
Isaac Newton sends greetings

As I did not reply at once on receipt of your letter, it slipped from my hands and was long mislaid among my papers, and I could not lay hands on it until yesterday. This vexed me since I value your friendship very highly and have for many years considered you as one of the leading geometers of this century, as I have also acknowledged on every occasion that offered. For although I do my best to avoid philosophical and mathematical correspondences, I was however afraid that our friendship might be diminished by silence, and at the very moment too when our friend Wallis has inserted into his imminent new edition of his *History of Algebra*[8] some new points from letters which I once wrote to you by the hand of Mr. Oldenburg,[9] and so has given me a handle to write to you on that question also. For he asked me to reveal a certain double method which I had there concealed by transposed letters. And so I have been compelled to expound as briefly as possible my method of fluxions which I had concealed by this sentence: *given an equation involving any number of fluent quantities to find the fluxions, and conversely.* I hope indeed that I have written nothing to displease you, and if there is anything that you think deserves censure, please let me know of it by letter, since I value friends more highly than mathematical discoveries . . . [.]

Huygens is a master, and his remarks on my discoveries are brilliant.[10] The parallax of the sun is less than I had concluded it to be;[11] and it would seem [in his view] the motion of sounds is perhaps more rectilinear. But some very fine matter seems to fill the heavens. For since celestial motions are more regular than if they arose from vortices and observe other laws, so much so that vortices contribute not to the regulation but the disturbance of the motions of planets and comets; and since all phenomena of the heavens and of the sea follow precisely, so far as I am aware, from nothing

---

[8] John Wallis's *A Treatise on Algebra, both Historical and Practical* (1685) appeared in a Latin edition as *De Algebra Tractatus: Historicus et Practicus* in 1693 from an Oxford publisher.

[9] Newton wrote a letter on 24 October 1676, a portion of which he had Oldenburg send to Leibniz.

[10] This refers to Huygens's *Treatise on Light*, which Leibniz mentions in his letter to Newton above (see n. 2 above).

[11] Newton discusses this issue in the first paragraph of his fourth letter to Bentley (see p. 102 of this volume).

but gravity acting in accordance with the laws described by me; and since nature is very simple, I have myself concluded that all other causes are to be rejected and that the heavens are to be stripped as far as may be of all matter, lest the motions of planets and comets be hindered or rendered irregular. But if, meanwhile, someone explains gravity along with all its laws by the action of some subtle matter, and shows that the motion of planets and comets will not be disturbed by this matter, I shall be far from objecting. As for the phenomena of colors, the so-called apparent colors as well as the fixed, I conceive myself to have discovered the surest explanation, but I refrain from publishing books for fear that disputes and controversies may be raised against me by ignoramuses.[12] The Newton whose works meet your eye in the catalogues of published books is someone else. My aim in these pages has been to give proof that I am your most sincere friend and that I value your friendship very highly. Farewell.

LEIBNIZ TO HARTSOEKER PUBLISHED IN
MEMOIRS OF LITERATURE
Hanover, 10 February 1711

You speak, sir, as if you knew not what I mean by *conspiring motions*; and ask, whether what I call so, be not the same thing with rest? I answer, it is not. For rest does not tend to make or preserve the cohesion of the parts that are at rest; and though two bodies remain one by another, they make no effort to continue to remain together, whether they touch one another, or not: but when there is a *conspiring motion* in their parts, which is disturbed by a separation, some strength is required to overcome that obstacle. Nor is it necessary that in the *conspiring motions* the parts should not change their distance. They may very well change it, provided that spontaneous change be quite another thing than a violent change, which would occasion a separation, and disturb those motions: and the parts of bodies resist a separation, not because they have a tendency to be divided; for in such a case they would resist still, if they were altogether at rest, which is contrary to what I maintain; but because they have a considerable motion, which must be disturbed by a separation. If those parts tend to a separation of themselves, they help any one who would separate them;

---

[12] Newton is presumably referring here to his discussion of colors in his optical papers from the 1670s. The "book" he wrote on this and related topics, the *Opticks*, was not published until 1704.

but when they do not help him, it does not follow that they make an opposition, and some positive cause is requisite for that.

I own that some force is requisite to expel a body from its place, or to make it go faster than it would do of itself; but if the body D tends to drive the body C from its place, the resistance of the body C, which lessens the swiftness of the body D, has nothing in it; from whence it may be inferred that the body B, though nothing tends to drive it out, ought to accompany the body C, whether the interval between B and C be great or small, or none at all. We must therefore suppose, in order to produce that union between B and C, or their going along together, some other reasons than rest, or the situation of the one by the other; but because it ought to proceed from the mechanism, I can find it nowhere but in the *conspiring motion*, common to some parts of the bodies B and C, which conveys some parts from the one into the other by a kind of circulation, and which must be disturbed by the separation of the bodies.

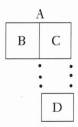

To say that the *conspiring motions* are a fiction, is the same as to say, that every motion is a fiction. For, sir, how will you make a motion unless there be some relation among the motions of the parts? The very nature of fluids in agitation leads them to those motions that are most fitting.

You say your atoms have no parts; and you think it strange that I should suppose one may conceive that an atom A has two parts B and C. But are you not obliged to own, that one may conceive that an atom D goes against the atom A, without going directly against the part B; and in such a manner that it would carry C along with it, and leave B, if A was not an atom, or a solid body? There is therefore some reason to affirm, that the pretended atom is not without parts. You must assign the causes of its *atomity*,[13] if I may so speak, that is, why D cannot carry C along with it,

---

[13] Leibniz coins a term here, but perhaps his meaning is plain.

without carrying B at the same time; and you must find a strong glue to make one of those parts stick to the other, if you are not willing to have recourse to the *conspiring motion.*

If you allege only the will of God for it, you have recourse to a miracle, and even to a perpetual miracle; for the will of God works through a miracle, whenever we are not able to account for that will and its effects from the nature of the objects. For example, if any one should say, it is God's will that a planet should move round in its orbit, without any other cause of its motion, I maintain, that it would be a perpetual miracle: for by the nature of things, the planet going round tends to remove from its orbit through the tangent, if nothing hinders it; and God must continually prevent it, if no natural cause does it. The same ought to be said of your atoms; for the body C will be naturally carried away by the body D, and the body B will not follow, if nothing hinders such a separation; and if you look out for the reason of it in the will of God, you must suppose a miracle.

It may be said in a very good sense that every thing is a continued miracle, that is, worthy of admiration: but it seems to me that the example of a planet which goes round and preserves its motion in its orbit without any other help but that of God, being compared with a planet kept in its orbit by the matter which constantly drives it towards the sun, plainly shows what difference there is between reasonable natural miracles, and those that are properly so called, or supernatural; or rather between a reasonable explication, and a fiction invented to support an ill-grounded opinion. Such is the method of those who say, after Mr. De Roberval's Aristarchus, that all bodies attract one another by a law of nature, which God made in the beginning of things.[14] For alleging nothing else to obtain such an effect, and admitting nothing that was made by God whereby it may appear how he attains to that end, they have recourse to a miracle, that is, to a supernatural thing, which continues forever, when the question is to find out a natural cause.

You are in the right, sir, when you say we ought frequently to acknowledge our ignorance, and that it is a wiser method than to run into nonsense, by pretending to account for those things, which we do not understand. But to own that we know not the causes of some effects, is a different

---

[14] See Giles Persone de Roberval, *Aristarchi Samii De Mundi Systemate, Partibus, et Motibus eiusdem Libellus* (Paris, 1644).

thing from affirming that there are some things of which no reason can be given, which is contrary to the first principles of reasoning: it is just as if somebody had denied the axiom, which Archimedes made use of in his book *de Aequiponderantibus*,[15] viz., that a balance, when everything is equal on both sides, remains in an *equilibrium*, under pretense that things are not sufficiently understood, and that perhaps the balance undergoes some alteration without any reason for it.

Thus the ancients and the moderns, who own that gravity is an *occult quality*, are in the right, if they mean by it that there is a certain mechanism unknown to them, whereby all bodies tend towards the center of the earth. But if they mean that the thing is performed without any mechanism by a simple *primitive quality*, or by a law of God, who produces that effect without using any intelligible means, it is an unreasonable occult quality, and so very occult, that it is impossible it should ever be clear, though an angel, or God himself, should undertake to explain it.

The same ought to be said of *hardness*. If any one acknowledges that the mechanism, which occasions hardness, is unknown to him, he is in the right; but if he pretends that hardness proceeds from any other cause than mechanism, and if he has recourse to a primitive hardness, as the assertors of atoms do, he recurs to a quality that is so occult, that it can never be made clear; that is, to a thing both unreasonable and contrary to the first principles of reasoning, since he owns that there are some natural things that have no natural cause.

Those are also guilty of the same fault who admit an indifference of *equilibrium*, as if the will could be determined, when all things are equal on both sides both inwardly and outwardly. Such a case never happens: there is always a greater inclination on one side than on the other; and the will is always inclined by some reason, or disposition, without being necessitated; and I dare say that many faults committed in arguing proceed from not duly observing this great principle, *that nothing happens without a sufficient season for it*. A principle, the force and consequences whereof have not been sufficiently considered by Descartes, and many other great men. That principle is sufficient to destroy the *vacuum*, the atoms, and the occult qualities of some philosophers, and even the first element of Descartes, with his globes, and many other fictions.

---

[15] Leibniz may have had this edition of Archimedes in mind: *Archimedous Panta Sozomena.* = *Archimedis Opera quae Extant: Novis Demonstrationibus Commentariisque Illustrata*, ed. David Rivault Flurance (Paris, 1615).

Thus, sir, you see why God could not create atoms, that is, bodies hard by their own nature, bodies of a primitive and insuperable hardness not to be accounted for; as he could not create planets that should move round of themselves, without any cause that should prevent their removing through the tangent: for a miracle at least must keep the planet in, and prevent the separation of the parts of the hard body, if a mechanical or intelligible cause does not do it. Granting the possibility of atoms, and the impossibility of a *vacuum*, I don't see why we should be forced to have recourse to a first element, that is, to a matter altogether fluid. Why may we not suppose space to be filled up with a matter that has different degrees of fluidity and tenacity, as I believe it is the nature of all matter?

Nor do I see why hard bodies should necessarily receive all their motion from fluid bodies, especially from a mass altogether fluid, or from our first element. For all matter being equally susceptible of motion, and equally incapable of producing it in itself, the most solid bodies may receive it, as well as those that are most fluid. Nay, it might be said, that the motion communicated to some few hard bodies may serve to account for the motion of many fluid bodies; and consequently, that it is anterior in order. For a solid body, thrown into a fluid, puts it into motion and produces a kind of circulation necessary to fill up the place which otherwise would remain empty behind the solid body; and that circulation forms a kind of vortex that has some affinity with that which we conceive round the lodestone [i.e. magnet].

It ought not to be said, that the universe is like an animal endued with life and intelligence: for then one might be apt to believe that God is the soul of that animal; whereas he is *intelligentia supramundana*, and the cause of the world: and if the universe was unlimited, it would be a collection of animals and other beings, but it could not be a single animal.

Your first element is not more susceptible of life and intelligence than any other bulk of matter; and since it is not organized, it is not fit it should have any perception, which must always answer the actions of organs, if you will have nature to act orderly and coherently.

You say, sir, that it is impossible for us to apprehend how a substance comes to have life and perception: and you are in the right, when the question is about particulars and the beginning of things. But perhaps you will own that the thing is more intelligible in my system of the *pre-established harmony*, by conceiving that our spiritual substances do naturally represent what happens in that part of matter to which they are united.

I have sufficiently answered those who objected to me that such a system was inconsistent with *free will*; for God knowing what men's minds would freely choose in time, adapted their bodies to it before hand. Mr. Jaquelot, who raised such an objection against me by word of mouth, was satisfied with my answer, as he owned in his book against Mr. Bayle: nay, he has cleared it with an elegant comparison. I have answered Father Lami's objection in the same manner; and my answer has been inserted in the *Journal des Sçavans*. When Mr. Bernoulli was Professor at Groningen, he maintained some theses, wherein he vindicated my opinion concerning the *pre-established harmony*.[16]

To conclude, the imperfections observable in the universe are like the dissonances of an excellent piece of music, which contribute to render it more perfect, in the opinion of the best judges. And therefore it cannot be said that when God created the world he made an imperfect machine. It is true, there are some machines in this world, that have not always, and from the beginning, [had] all the perfection that they are capable of.

I return you many thanks, sir, for your good wishes about the beginning of the New Year; and I wish you may long contribute to the improvement of the sciences, being with great zeal,

SIR,
Your most humble, and most obedient servant,
Leibniz

NEWTON TO THE EDITOR OF THE *MEMOIRS OF LITERATURE*, UNPUBLISHED
London, circa May 1712

Sir
In your weekly paper dated 5 May 1712 I meet with two letters, one written by Mr. Leibniz to Mr. Hartsoeker, the other by Mr. Hartsoeker to Mr. Leibniz in answer to the former. And in the letter of Mr. Leibniz I meet with some things reflecting upon the English; I hope you will do them

---

[16] See M. Jaquelot, *Entretiens de Maxime et de Themiste, ou, Reponse à l'Examen de la Theologie de Mr. Bayle* (Rotterdam, 1707); Pierre Bayle's most famous work is the *Dictionnaire Historique et Critique* (Rotterdam, 1697). Bayle and Leibniz were famous interlocutors. Due to François Lami's criticisms of Leibniz's conception of the pre-established harmony, Leibniz wrote a draft of a reply to Lami in 1702. Leibniz also corresponded in the fall of 1698 with the mathematician and physicist Johann Bernoulli.

the justice to publish this vindication as you have printed the reflexion. He writes thus: "It may be said in a very good sense that every thing is a continual miracle, that is, worthy of admiration, but it seems to me that the example of a planet which goes round and preserves it[s] motion in its orbit without any other help but that of God, being compared with a planet kept in its orbit by that matter which constantly drives it toward the sun, plainly shows what difference there is between reasonable natural miracles and those that are properly so called or supernatural; or rather between a reasonable explication, and a fiction invented to support an ill-grounded opinion. Such is the method of those who say, after Mr. de Roberval's Aristarchus,[17] that all bodies attract one another by a law of nature which God made in the beginning of things. For alleging nothing else to obtain such an effect and admitting nothing that was made by God whereby it may appear how he attains to that end, they have recourse to a miracle, that is, to a supernatural thing, which continues forever, when the question is to find out a natural cause."[18] Thus far Mr. Leibniz. I know not what just occasion there was for this reflexion in a discourse foreign to this matter, but it's plain this was intended against some in England and I hope to make it as plain that it was undeserved. For the true state of the case is this. It has been proved by some that all bodies upon the surface of the earth gravitate toward the earth in proportion to the quantity of matter in each of them; that the moon tends toward the earth and all the planets toward one another by the same law; and that by this tendency all their motions are performed. These things have been proved by mathematical demonstrations grounded upon experiments and the phenomena of nature: and Mr. Leibniz himself cannot deny that they have been proved. But he objects that because *they allege nothing else to obtain such an effect* (he means a tendency of all bodies towards one another) *besides a law of nature which God made in the beginning of things and admit nothing that was made by God* (he means no vortices) *whereby it may appear how God attains to that end, they have recourse to a miracle, and that is, to a supernatural thing which continues for ever, when the question is to find out a natural cause.* Because they do not explain gravity by a

---

[17] See n. 14 above.

[18] Each of Newton's paraphrases of Leibniz's original letter is very nearly exact; they have not been altered to correspond exactly to Leibniz's text, except in the case of the phrase "reasonable natural miracles," which I have altered both in the original and in Newton's quotation to match Leibniz's original French.

mechanical hypothesis, he charges them with making it a supernatural thing, a miracle and a fiction invented to support an ill-grounded opinion and compares their method of philosophy to that of Mr. de Roberval's Aristarchus, which is all one as to call it romantic [i.e. fictional]. They show that there is a universal gravity and that all the phenomena of the heavens are the effect of it and with the cause of gravity they meddle not but leave it to be found out by them that can explain it, whether mechanically or otherwise. And doth it deserve to be scouted with the language of a supernatural thing, a miracle, a fiction invented to support an ill-grounded opinion, and a method of philosophy after Mr. Roberval's romance?

But Mr. Leibniz goes on. "The ancients and the moderns, who own that gravity is an occult quality, are in the right, if they mean by it that there is a certain mechanism unknown to them whereby all bodies tend towards the center of the earth. But if they mean that the thing is performed without any mechanism by a simple primitive quality or by a law of God who produces that effect without using any intelligible means, it is an unreasonable and occult quality, and so very occult that it is impossible that it should ever be done though an angel or God himself should undertake to explain it." The same ought to be said of hardness. So then gravity and hardness must go for unreasonable occult qualities unless they can be explained mechanically. And why may not the same be said of the *vis inertiae* [force of inertia] and the extension, the duration and mobility of bodies, and yet no man ever attempted to explain these qualities mechanically, or took them for miracles or supernatural things or fictions or occult qualities. They are the natural, real, reasonable, manifest qualities of all bodies seated in them by the will of God from the beginning of the creation and perfectly incapable of being explained mechanically, and so may be the hardness of primitive particles of bodies. And therefore if any man should say that bodies attract one another by a power whose cause is unknown to us, or by a power seated in the frame of nature by the will of God, or by a power seated in a substance in which bodies move and float without resistance and which has therefore no *vis inertiae* but acts by other laws than those that are mechanical: I know not why he should be said to introduce miracles and occult qualities and fictions into the world. For Mr. Leibniz himself will scarce say that thinking is mechanical as it must be if to explain it otherwise be to make a miracle, an occult quality, and a fiction.

But he goes on and tells us that God *could not create planets that* should move round of themselves without any cause that should prevent their removing through the tangent. For a miracle at least must keep *the planet in*. But certainly God could create planets that should move round of themselves without any other cause than gravity that should prevent their removing through the tangent. For gravity without a miracle may keep the planets in. And to understand this without knowing the cause of gravity, is as good a progress in philosophy as to understand the frame of a clock and the dependence of the wheels upon one another without knowing the cause of the gravity of the weight which moves the machine is in the philosophy of clockwork; or the understanding of the frame of the bones and muscles and their connection in the body of an animal and how the bones are moved by the contracting or dilating of the muscles without knowing how the muscles are contracted or dilated by the power of the mind, is [in] the philosophy of animal motion.

VI

Correspondence with Roger Cotes [1713]

NEWTON TO COTES

London, 28 March 1713

Sir

I had your [letter] of Feb 18th, and the difficulty you mention which lies in these words "And since, by the third law of motion, every attraction is mutual" is removed by considering that as in geometry the word "hypothesis" is not taken in so large a sense as to include the axioms and postulates, so in experimental philosophy it is not to be taken in so large a sense as to include the first principles or axioms which I call the laws of motion. These principles are deduced from phenomena and made general by induction: which is the highest evidence that a proposition can have in this philosophy. And the word "hypothesis" is here used by me to signify only such a proposition as is not a phenomenon nor deduced from any phenomena but assumed or supposed without any experimental proof. Now the mutual and mutually equal attraction of bodies is a branch of the third law of motion and how this branch is deduced from phenomena you may see in the end of the corollaries of the laws of motion, page 22.[1] If a body attracts another body contiguous to it and is not mutually attracted by the other: the attracted body will drive the other before it and both will go away together with an accelerated motion *in infinitum*, as it were by a self-moving principle, contrary to the first law of motion, whereas there is no such phenomenon in all nature.

---

[1] See p. 83 in this volume.

At the end of the last paragraph but two now ready to be printed off I desire you to add after the words "and a God without dominion, providence, and final causes is nothing other than fate and nature" these words: "This concludes the discussion of God, and to treat of God from phenomena is certainly a part of natural philosophy."

And for preventing exceptions against the use of the word "hypothesis" I desire you to conclude the next paragraph in this manner: "For whatever is not deduced from the phenomena must be called a hypothesis; and hypotheses, whether metaphysical or physical, or based on occult qualities, or mechanical, have no place in experimental philosophy. In this experimental philosophy, propositions are deduced from the phenomena and are made general by induction. The impenetrability, mobility, and impetus of bodies, and the laws of motion and the law of gravity have been found by this method. And it is enough that gravity really exists and acts according to the laws that we have set forth and is sufficient to explain all the motions of the heavenly bodies and of our sea."[2]

I have not time to finish this letter but intend to write to you again on Tuesday.

I am, your most humble Servant
Is. NEWTON
For the Reverend Mr Roger Cotes
Professor of Astronomy, at his Chamber in Trinity College in Cambridge.

NEWTON TO COTES
Unsent Draft: Circa March 1713

Sir

I like your design of adding something more particularly concerning the manner of philosophizing made use of in the *Principia* and wherein it differs from the method of others, viz. by deducing things mathematically from principles derived from phenomena by induction. These principles are the three laws of motion. And these laws in being deduced from phenomena by induction and backed with reason and the three general rules of philosophizing are distinguished from hypotheses and considered

---

[2] In all three cases, Newton gives the passages and additions in Latin.

as axioms. Upon these are founded all the propositions in the first and second book. And these propositions are in the third book applied to the motions of the heavenly bodies.

And first because the planets move in curve[d] lines, it follows from the first axiom or law of nature that they are incessantly acted upon by some force which continually diverts them from a rectilinear course.

Again from propositions 2 and 3 [of] Book One, it follows that this force is directed towards the central bodies about which the planets move.

And by proposition 6, corollary 4 of Book One, and proposition 45, corollary 1 of Book One, that this force in receding from the central body decreases in a duplicate proportion of the distance. Etc.

And when you come at the difficulty you mention in the first corollary of the fifth proposition of the third book, which lies in these words "And since, by the third law of motion, every attraction is mutual": the objection you mention may be proposed and answered in this manner. (1) That it is but an hypothesis not founded upon any one observation. (2) That it is attended with the absurd consequence described [on] page 22, namely that a body attracted by another body without mutually attracting it would go to the other body and drive it away before it with an accelerated motion *in infinitum*, contrary to the first law of motion. And such an absurd hypothesis, which would disturb all nature, is not to be admitted in opposition to the first and third laws of motion which are grounded upon phenomena. For that all attraction is mutual and mutually equal follows from both those laws. One may suppose that bodies may by an unknown power be perpetually accelerated and so reject the first law of motion. One may suppose that God can create a penetrable body and so reject the impenetrability of matter. But to admit of such hypotheses in opposition to rational propositions founded upon phenomena by induction is to destroy all arguments taken from phenomena by induction and all principles founded upon such arguments. And therefore as I regard not hypotheses in explaining the phenomena of nature, so I regard them not in opposition to arguments founded upon phenomena by induction or to principles settled upon such arguments. In arguing for any principle or proposition from phenomena by induction, hypotheses are not to be considered. The argument holds good till some phenomenon can be produced against it. This argument holds good by the third rule of philosophizing. And if we break that rule, we cannot affirm any one general law of nature: we cannot so much as affirm that all matter is impenetrable. Experimental philosophy reduces phenomena to general rules and looks upon the rules to be general when they hold generally in phenomena. It is not enough to object that a contrary phenomenon may happen but to make a legitimate objection, a contrary phenomenon must be actually produced. Hypothetical philosophy consists in imaginary explications of things and imaginary arguments for or against such explications, or against the arguments of experimental philosophers founded upon induction. The first sort of philosophy is followed by me, the latter too much by Descartes, Leibniz, and some others. And according to the first sort of philosophy the three laws of motion are proposed as general principles of philosophy though founded upon phenomena by no better argument than that of induction without exception of any one phenomenon. For the impenetrability of matter is grounded upon no better an argument. And the mutual equality of attraction (which is a branch of the third law of motion) is backed by this further argument, that is, if the attraction between two bodies was not mutual and mutually equal they would not stay *in rerum natura* [in the natural world]. The body which is most strongly attracted would go to the other and press upon it, and by the excess of its pressure both would go away together with a motion accelerated *in infinitum*. If a great mountain upon either pole of the earth gravitated towards the rest of the earth more than the rest of the earth gravitated towards the mountain, the weight of the mountain would drive the earth from the plane of the ecliptic and cause it, so soon as it could extricate itself from the system of the sun and planets, to go away *in infinitum* with a motion perpetually accelerated. Thus the objection which you mention is not only an hypothesis and on that account to be excluded [from] experimental philosophy, but also introduces a principle of self-motion into bodies which would disturb the whole frame of nature, and in the general opinion of mankind is as remote from the nature of matter as impenetrability [read: penetrability] is reckoned to be. Experimental philosophy argues only from phenomena, draws general conclusions from the consent of phenomena, and looks upon the conclusion as general when the consent is general without exception, though the generality cannot be demonstrated a priori. In mathematics all propositions not demonstrated mathematically are hypotheses, but some are admitted as principles under the name of axioms or postulates without being called hypotheses. So in experimental philosophy it's proper to distinguish propositions into principles, propositions, and hypotheses, calling those propositions which are deduced from phenomena by proper arguments and made general by induction (the best way of arguing in philosophy for a general proposition) and those hypotheses which are not deduced from phenomena by proper arguments. But if any man will take the word "hypothesis" in a larger sense, he may extend it, if he pleases, to the impenetrability of matter, the laws of motion, and the axioms of geometers. For it is not worth the while to dispute about the signification of a word.

What has been said, doth not hinder the body B from being moved by an invisible hand towards the resting body A: [ends].

VII

An Account of the Book Entitled *Commercium Epistolicum* [1715]

The philosophy which Mr Newton in his *Principles* and *Opticks* has pursued is experimental; and it is not the business of experimental philosophy to teach the causes of things any further than they can be proved by experiments. We are not to fill this philosophy with opinions which cannot be proved by phenomena. In this philosophy hypotheses have no place, unless as conjectures or questions proposed to be examined by experiments. For this reason, Mr Newton in his *Opticks* distinguished those things which were made certain by experiments from those things which remained uncertain, and which he therefore proposed in the end of his *Opticks* in the form of queries. For this reason, in the preface to his *Principles,* when he had mentioned the motions of the planets, comets, moon and sea as deduced in this book from gravity, he added: "If only we could derive the other phenomena of nature from mechanical principles by the same kind of reasoning! For many things lead me to have a suspicion that all phenomena may depend on certain forces by which the particles of bodies, by causes not yet known, either are impelled towards one another and cohere in regular figures, or are repelled from one another and recede. Since these forces are unknown, philosophers have hitherto made trial of nature in vain." And in the end of this book in the second edition, he said that for want of a sufficient number of experiments, he forbore to describe the laws of the actions of the spirit or agent by which this attraction is performed. And for the same reason he is silent about the cause of gravity, there occurring no experiments or phenomena by which he might prove what was the cause thereof. And this he hath abundantly declared in his *Principles*, near the beginning thereof, in these words: "I am not now considering the physical causes and sites of forces" [definition 8]. And a little after: "Moreover, I use interchangeably and indiscriminately words signifying attraction, impulse, or any sort of propensity towards a centre, considering these forces not from a physical but only from a mathematical point of view. Therefore, let the reader beware of thinking that by words of this kind I am anywhere defining a species or mode of action or a physical cause or reason, or that I am attributing forces in a true and physical sense to centres (which are mathematical points) if I happen to say that centres attract or that centres have forces." And in the end of his *Opticks*: "How these attractions [viz. gravitational, magnetic, & electrical] may be performed, I do not here consider. What I call attraction may be performed by impulse, or by some other means unknown to me. I use "attraction" here to signify only in general any force by which bodies tend towards one another, whatsoever be the cause. For we must learn from the phenomena of nature what bodies attract one another, and what are the laws and properties of the attraction, before we enquire the cause by which the attraction is performed." And a little after he mentions the same attractions as forces which by phenomena appear to have a being in nature, though their causes be not yet known; and distinguishes them from the occult qualities which are supposed to flow from the specific forms of things. And in the Scholium at the end of his *Principles*, after he had mentioned the properties of gravity, he added: "I have not as yet been able to deduce from phenomena the reason for these properties of gravity, and I do not feign hypotheses. For whatever is not deduced from the phenomena must be called a hypothesis; and hypotheses, whether metaphysical or physical, or based on occult qualities, have no place in experimental philosophy . . . And it is enough that gravity really exists and acts according to the laws that we have set forth and is sufficient to explain all the motions of the heavenly bodies and of our sea." And after all this, one would wonder that Mr Newton should be reflected upon for not explaining the causes of gravity and other attractions by hypotheses; as if it were a crime to content himself with certainties and let uncertainties alone. And yet the editors of the *Acta Eruditorum*: (a) have told the world that Mr Newton denies that the cause of gravity is mechanical, and that if the spirit or agent by which electrical attraction is performed be not the aether or subtle matter of Descartes, it is less valuable than an hypothesis, and perhaps may be the hylarchic principle of Dr Henry

More;[1] and Mr. Leibniz: (b) hath accused him of making gravity a natural or essential property of bodies, and an occult quality and miracle. And by this sort of raillery they are persuading the Germans that Mr Newton wants judgment, and was not able to invent the infinitesimal method [the calculus].

It must be allowed that these two gentlemen differ very much in philosophy. The one proceeds upon the evidence arising from experiments and phenomena, and stops where such evidence is wanting; the other is taken up with hypotheses, and propounds them, not to be examined by experiments, but to be believed without examination. The one for want of experiments to decide the question doth not affirm whether the cause of gravity be mechanical or not mechanical: the other that it is a perpetual miracle if it be not mechanical. The one (by way of enquiry) attributes it to the power of the creator that the least particles of matter are hard: the other attributes the hardness of matter to conspiring motions, and calls it a perpetual miracle if the cause of this hardness be other than mechanical. The one doth not affirm that animal motion in man is purely mechanical: the other teaches that it is purely mechanical, the soul or mind (according to the hypothesis of a pre-established harmony) never acting upon the body so as to alter or influence its motions. The one teaches that God (the God in whom we live and move and have our being)[2] is omnipresent, but not as a soul of the world: the other that he is not the soul of the world, but INTELLIGENTIA SUPRAMUNDANA, an intelligence above the bounds of the world; whence it seems to follow that he cannot do any thing within the bounds of the world, unless by an incredible miracle. The one teaches that philosophers are to argue from phenomena and experiments to the causes thereof, and thence to the causes of those causes, and so on till we come to the first cause: the other that all the actions of the first cause are miracles, and all the laws impressed on nature by the will of God are perpetual miracles and occult qualities, and therefore not to be considered in philosophy. But must the constant and universal laws of nature, if derived from the power of God or the action of a cause not yet known to us, be called miracles and occult qualities, that is to say, wonders and absurdities? Must all the arguments for a God taken from

---

[1] Henry More was an important Cambridge Platonist whose work influenced Newton while he was a student at Trinity College in the 1660s. The "hylarchic" principle is said to be a type of non-material agent that would somehow control material bodies.
[2] Newton quotes here a passage from Acts (17: 28) that was often cited in this period.

the phenomena of nature be exploded by new hard names? And must experimental philosophy be exploded as miraculous and absurd because it asserts nothing more than can be proved by experiments, and we cannot yet prove by experiments that all the phenomena in nature can be solved by mere mechanical causes? Certainly these things deserve to be better considered.

VIII

Queries to the *Opticks* [1721]

Query 28.

[. . .] And against filling the heavens with fluid mediums, unless they be exceeding rare, a great objection arises from the regular and very lasting motions of the planets and comets in all manner of courses through the heavens. For thence it is manifest, that the heavens are void of all sensible resistance, and by consequence of all sensible matter.[1]

For the resisting power of fluid mediums arises partly from the attrition of the parts of the medium, and partly from the *vis inertiae* [force of inertia] of the matter. That part of the resistance of a spherical body which arises from the attrition of the parts of the medium is very nearly as the diameter, or at the most, as the *factum* [factor] of the diameter, and the velocity of the spherical body together. And that part of the resistance which arises from the *vis inertiae* of the matter, is as the square of that *factum*. And by this difference the two sorts of resistance may be distinguished from one another in any medium; and these being distinguished, it will be found that almost all the resistance of bodies of a competent magnitude moving in air, water, quicksilver, and such like fluids with a competent velocity, arises from the *vis inertiae* of the parts of the fluid.

Now that part of the resisting power of any medium which arises from the tenacity, friction, or attrition of the parts of the medium, may be diminished by dividing the matter into smaller parts, and making the parts more smooth and slippery: but that part of the resistance which arises from the *vis inertiae* is proportional to the density of the matter, and cannot be

---

[1] Newton also discusses this issue in his letter to Leibniz of 1693 (p. 108 above) and in the General Scholium to the *Principia* (p. 89 above).

127

diminished by dividing the matter into smaller parts, nor by any other means than by decreasing the density of the medium. And for these reasons the density of fluid mediums is very nearly proportional to their resistance. Liquors [i.e. liquids] which differ not much in density, as water, spirit of wine, spirit of turpentine, hot oil, differ not much in resistance. Water is thirteen or fourteen times lighter than quicksilver, and by consequence thirteen or fourteen times rarer, and its resistance is less than that of quicksilver in the same proportion, or thereabouts, as I have found by experiments made with pendulums. The open air in which we breathe is eight or nine hundred times lighter than water, and by consequence eight or nine hundred times rarer, and accordingly its resistance is less than that of water in the same proportion, or thereabouts; as I have also found by experiments made with pendulums. And in thinner air the resistance is still less, and at length, by rarefying the air becomes insensible. For small feathers falling in the open air meet with great resistance, but in a tall glass well emptied of air, they fall as fast as lead or gold, as I have seen tried several times. Whence the resistance seems still to decrease in proportion to the density of the fluid. For I do not find by any experiments that bodies moving in quicksilver, water, or air, meet with any other sensible resistance than what arises from the density and tenacity of those sensible fluids, as they would do if the pores of those fluids, and all other spaces, were filled with a dense and subtle fluid. Now if the resistance in a vessel well emptied of air was but a hundred times less than in the open air, it would be about a million times less than in quicksilver [mercury]. But it seems to be much less in such a vessel, and still much less in the heavens, at the height of three or four hundred miles from the earth, or above. For Mr Boyle has showed that air may be rarefied above ten thousand times in vessels of glass; and the heavens are much emptier of air than any *vacuum* we can make below. For since the air is compressed by the weight of the incumbent atmosphere, and the density of air is proportional to the force compressing it, it follows by computation that at the height of about seven and a half English miles from the earth, the air is four times rarer than at the surface of the earth; and at the height of 15 miles it is sixteen times rarer than that at the surface of the earth; and at the height of $22^{1/2}$, 30, or 38 miles, it is respectively 64, 256, or 1024 times rarer, or thereabouts; and at the height of 76, 152, 228 miles, it is about 1,000,000, 1,000,000,000,000, or 1,000,000,000,000,000,000 times rarer; and so on.

Heat promotes fluidity very much by diminishing the tenacity of bodies. It makes many bodies fluid which are not fluid in cold, and increases the fluidity of tenacious liquids, as of oil, balsam, and honey, and thereby decreases their resistance. But it decreases not the resistance of water considerably, as it would do if any considerable part of the resistance of water arose from the attrition or tenacity of its parts. And therefore the resistance of water arises principally and almost entirely from the *vis inertiae* of its matter; and by consequence, if the heavens were as dense as water, they would not have much less resistance than water; if as dense as quicksilver, they would not have much less resistance than quicksilver; if absolutely dense, or full of matter without any vacuum, let the matter be never so subtle and fluid, they would have a greater resistance than quicksilver. A solid globe in such a medium would lose above half its motion in moving three times the length of its diameter, and a globe not solid (such as are the planets) would be retarded sooner. And therefore to make way for the regular and lasting motions of the planets and comets, it's necessary to empty the heavens of all matter, except perhaps some very thin vapours, steams, or effluvia [discharges], arising from the atmospheres of the earth, planets, and comets, and from such an exceedingly rare aethereal medium as we described above. A dense fluid can be of no use for explaining the phenomena of nature, the motions of the planets and comets being better explained without it. It serves only to disturb and retard the motions of those great bodies, and make the frame of nature languish: and in the pores of bodies, it serves only to stop the vibrating motions of their parts, wherein their heat and activity consists.[2] And as it is of no use, and hinders the operations of nature, and makes her languish, so there is no evidence for its existence, and therefore it ought to be rejected. And if it be rejected, the hypotheses that light consists in pression [pressure] or motion, propagated through such a medium, are rejected with it.[3]

And for rejecting such a medium, we have the authority of those the oldest and most celebrated philosophers of Greece and Phoenicia, who made a *vacuum*, and atoms, and the gravity of atoms, the first principles

---

[2] Cf. Newton's letter to Leibniz of 1693 on p. 108 of this volume.

[3] Newton discussed this hypothesis early in his career in the papers in optics. In his 1672 paper, for instance, he writes of other "mechanical hypotheses on which light is supposed to be caused by any pression or motion whatsoever, excited in the aether by the agitated parts of luminous bodies": *Philosophical Transactions* 7 (1672): 5089.

of their philosophy; tacitly attributing gravity to some other cause than dense matter. Later philosophers banish the consideration of such a cause out of natural philosophy, feigning hypotheses for explaining all things mechanically, and referring other causes to metaphysics: whereas the main business of natural philosophy is to argue from phenomena without feigning hypotheses, and to deduce causes from effects, till we come to the very first cause, which certainly is not mechanical; and not only to unfold the mechanism of the world, but chiefly to resolve these and such like questions.

What is there in places almost empty of matter, and whence is it that the sun and planets gravitate towards one another, without dense matter between them? Whence is it that nature doth nothing in vain; and whence arises all that order and beauty which we see in the world? To what end are comets, and whence is it that planets move all one and the same way in orbits concentric, while comets move all manner of ways in orbits very eccentric; and what hinders the fixed stars from falling upon one another? How came the bodies of animals to be contrived with so much art, and for what ends were their several parts? Was the eye contrived without skill in optics, and the ear without knowledge of sounds? How do the motions of the body follow from the will, and whence is the instinct in animals? Is not the sensory of animals that place to which the sensitive substance is present, and into which the sensible species of things are carried through the nerves and brain, that there they may be perceived by their immediate presence to that substance? And these things being rightly dispatched, does it not appear from phenomena that there is a being incorporeal, living, intelligent, omnipresent, who in infinite space, as it were in his sensory,[4] sees the things themselves intimately, and thoroughly perceives them, and comprehends them wholly by their immediate presence to himself: of which things the images only carried through the organs of sense into our little sensoriums, are there seen and beheld by that which in us perceives and thinks. And though every true step made in this philosophy brings us not immediately to the knowledge of the first cause, yet it brings us nearer to it, and on that account is to be highly valued.

---

4 This phrase, which did not appear with the qualification "as it were" in some copies of the *Opticks*, was the centerpiece of a controversy between the Newtonians (especially Samuel Clarke) and Leibniz. See Alexandre Koyré and I. Bernard Cohen, "The Case of the Missing *Tanquam*," *Isis* 52: 555–66.

Query 30.

Are not gross bodies and light convertible into one another, and may not bodies receive much of their activity from the particles of light which enter their composition? For all fixed bodies being heated emit light so long as they continue sufficiently hot, and light mutually stops in bodies as often as its rays strike upon their parts, as we showed above. I know no body less apt to shine than water; and yet water by frequent distillations changes into fixed earth, as Mr Boyle has tried; and then this earth being enabled to endure a sufficient heat, shines by heat like other bodies.

The changing of bodies into light, and light into bodies, is very conformable to the course of nature, which seems delighted with transmutations. Water, which is a very fluid tasteless salt, changes by heat into vapour, which is a sort of air, and by cold into ice, which is a hard, pellucid, brittle, fusible stone; and this stone returns into water by heat, and vapour returns into water by cold. Earth by heat becomes fire, and by cold returns into earth. Dense bodies by fermentation rarefy into several sorts of air, and this air by fermentation, and sometimes without it, returns into dense bodies. Mercury appears sometimes in the form of a fluid metal, sometimes in the form of a hard brittle metal, sometimes in the form of a corrosive pellucid salt called sublimate, sometimes in the form of a tasteless, pellucid, volatile white earth, called *mercurius dulcis*; or in that of a red opaque volatile earth, called cinnabar;[5] or in that of a red or white precipitate, or in that of a fluid salt; and in distillation it turns into vapour, and being agitated in a vacuum, it shines like fire. And after all these changes it returns again into its first form of mercury. Eggs grow from insensible magnitudes, and change into animals; tadpoles into frogs; and worms into flies. All birds, beasts, and fishes, insects, trees and other vegetables, with their several parts, grow out of water and watery tinctures and salts, and by putrefaction [decomposition] return again into watery substances. And water standing a few days in the open air, yields a tincture, which (like that of malt) by standing longer yields a sediment and a spirit, but before putrefaction is fit nourishment for animals and vegetables. And among such various and strange transmutations, why may not nature change bodies into light, and light into bodies?

[5] Sublimate is mercuric chloride ($HgCl_2$), *mercurius dulcis* is mercurous chloride (Hg_2Cl_2), and cinnabar is mercury sulfide (HgS).

Query 31.

Have not the small particles of bodies certain powers, virtues, or forces, by which they act at a distance, not only upon the rays of light for reflecting, refracting, and inflecting them, but also upon one another for producing a great part of the phenomena of nature? For it's well known, that bodies act one upon another by the attractions of gravity, magnetism, and electricity; and these instances show the tenor and course of nature, and make it not improbable but that there may be more attractive powers than these. Nature is very consonant and conformable to her self. How these attractions may be performed, I do not here consider. What I call attraction may be performed by impulse, or by some other means unknown to me. I use that word here to signify only in general any force by which bodies tend towards one another, whatsoever be the cause. For we must learn from the phenomena of nature what bodies attract one another, and what are the laws and properties of the attraction, before we enquire the cause by which the attraction is performed. The attractions of gravity, magnetism, and electricity, reach to very sensible distances, and so have been observed by vulgar eyes, and there may be others which reach to so small distances as hitherto escape observation; and perhaps electrical attraction may reach to such small distances, even without being excited by friction.
[. . .]

The parts of all homogeneal hard bodies which fully touch one another, stick together very strongly. And for explaining how this may be, some have invented hooked atoms, which is begging the question; and others tell us that bodies are glued together by rest, that is, by an occult quality, or rather by nothing; and others, that they stick together by conspiring motions, that is, by relative rest amongst themselves. I [would] rather infer from their cohesion that their particles attract one another by some force, which in immediate contact is exceeding strong, at small distances performs the chymical operations above mentioned, and reaches not far from the particles with any sensible effect.

All bodies seem to be composed of hard particles: for otherwise fluids would not congeal; as water, oils, vinegar, and spirit or oil of vitriol [sulphuric acid] do by freezing; mercury by fumes of lead; spirit of nitre and mercury, by dissolving the mercury and evaporating the flegm [liquid obtained by distillation]; spirit of wine and spirit of urine, by deflegming and mixing them; and spirit of urine and spirit of salt, by subliming them together to make sal-armoniac [ammonium chloride]. Even the rays of light seem to be hard bodies; for otherwise they would not retain different properties in their different sides. And therefore hardness may be reckoned the property of all uncompounded matter. At least, this seems to be as evident as the universal impenetrability of matter. For all bodies, so far as experience reaches, are either hard, or may be hardened; and we have no other evidence of universal impenetrability, besides a large experience without an experimental exception.[6] Now if compound bodies are so very hard as we find some of them to be, and yet are very porous, and consist of parts which are only laid together, the simple particles which are void of pores, and were never yet divided, must be much harder. For such hard particles being heaped up together, can scarce touch one another in more than a few points, and therefore must be separable by much less force than is requisite to break a solid particle, whose parts touch in all the space between them, without any pores or interstices to weaken their cohesion. And how such very hard particles which are only laid together and touch only in a few points, can stick together, and that so firmly as they do, without the assistance of something which causes them to be attracted or pressed towards one another, is very difficult to conceive. [. . .]

Now the smallest particles of matter may cohere by the strongest attractions, and compose bigger particles of weaker virtue; and many of these may cohere and compose bigger particles whose virtue is still weaker, and so on for diverse successions, until the progression end in the biggest particles on which the operations in chymistry, and the colours of natural bodies, depend and which by cohering compose bodies of a sensible magnitude. If the body is compact, and bends or yields inward to pression without any sliding of its parts, it is hard and elastic, returning to its figure with a force rising from the mutual attraction of its parts. If the parts slide upon one another, the body is malleable or soft. If they slip easily, and are of a fit size to be agitated by heat, and the heat is big enough to keep them in agitation, the body is fluid; and if it be apt to stick to things, it is humid; and the drops of every fluid affect a round figure by the mutual attraction of their parts, as the globe of the earth and sea affects a round figure by the mutual attraction of its parts by gravity.

---

[6] This is a paraphrase of one part of the third rule in the Rules for the Study of Natural Philosophy (this volume p. 87).

Since metals dissolved in acids attract but a small quantity of the acid, their attractive force can reach but to a small distance from them. And as in algebra, where affirmative quantities vanish and cease, there negative ones begin; so in mechanics, where attraction ceases, there a repulsive virtue ought to succeed. And that there is such a virtue, seems to follow from the reflexions and inflexions [bending] of the rays of light. For the rays are repelled by bodies in both these cases, without the immediate contact of the reflecting or inflecting body. It seems also to follow from the emission of light; the ray so soon as it is shaken off from a shining body by the vibrating motion of the parts of the body, and gets beyond the reach of attraction, being driven away with exceeding great velocity. For that force which is sufficient to turn it back in reflexion, may be sufficient to emit it. It seems also to follow from the production of air and vapour. The particles when they are shaken off from bodies by heat or fermentation, so soon as they are beyond the reach of the attraction of the body, recede from it, and also from one another with great strength, and keep at a distance, so as sometimes to take up above a million of times more space than they did before in the form of a dense body. Which vast contraction and expansion seems unintelligible, by feigning the particles of air to be springy and ramous [branching], or rolled up like hoops, or by any other means than a repulsive power. The particles of fluids which do not cohere too strongly, and are of such a smallness as renders them most susceptible of those agitations which keep liquors in a fluor [liquids in a fluid state], are most easily separated and rarefied into vapour, and in the language of the chymists, they are volatile, rarefying with an easy heat, and condensing with cold. But those which are grosser, and so less susceptible of agitation, or cohere by a stronger attraction, are not separated without a stronger heat, or perhaps not without fermentation. And these last are the bodies which chymists call fixed [non-volatile], and being rarefied by fermentation, become true permanent air; those particles receding from one another with the greatest force, and being most difficultly brought together, which upon contact cohere most strongly. And because the particles of permanent air are grosser, and arise from denser substances than those of vapours, thence it is that true air is more ponderous than vapour, and that a moist atmosphere is lighter than a dry one, quantity for quantity. From the same repelling power it seems to be that flies walk upon the water without wetting their feet; and that the object glasses of long telescopes lie upon one another without touching;

and that dry powders are difficultly made to touch one another so as to stick together, unless by melting them, or wetting them with water, which by exhaling may bring them together; and that two polished marbles, which by immediate contact stick together, are difficultly brought so close together as to stick.

And thus nature will be very conformable to herself and very simple, performing all the great motions of the heavenly bodies by the attraction of gravity which intercedes those bodies, and almost all the small ones of their particles by some other attractive and repelling powers which intercede the particles. The *vis inertiae* [inertial force] is a passive principle by which bodies persist in their motion or rest, receive motion in proportion to the force impressing it, and resist as much as they are resisted. By this principle alone there never could have been any motion in the world. Some other principle was necessary for putting bodies into motion; and now [that] they are in motion, some other principle is necessary for conserving the motion. For from the various composition of two motions, it is very certain that there is not always the same quantity of motion in the world. For if two globes joined by a slender rod revolve about their common centre of gravity with an uniform motion, while that centre moves on uniformly in a right line drawn in the plane of their circular motion, the sum of the motions of the two globes, as often as the globes are in the right line described by their common centre of gravity, will be bigger than the sum of their motions, when they are in a line perpendicular to that right line. By this instance it appears that motion may be got or lost. But by reason of the tenacity of fluids, and attrition of their parts, and the weakness of elasticity in solids, motion is much more apt to be lost than got, and is always upon the decay. For bodies which are either absolutely hard, or so soft as to be void of elasticity, will not rebound from one another. Impenetrability makes them only stop. If two equal bodies meet directly in a vacuum, they will by the laws of motion stop where they meet and lose all their motion, and remain in rest, unless they be elastic and receive new motion from their spring. If they have so much elasticity as suffices to make them rebound with a quarter, or half, or three quarters of the force with which they come together, they will lose three quarters, or half, or a quarter of their motion. And this may be tried, by letting two equal pendulums fall against one another from equal heights. If the pendulums be of lead or soft clay, they will lose all or almost all their motions: if of elastic bodies, they will lose all but what they recover from their elasticity. If it be said that they can lose no motion but what they communicate to other bodies, the consequence is that in a vacuum they can lose no motion, but when they meet they must go on and penetrate one another's dimensions. If three equal round vessels be filled, the one with water, the other with oil, the third with molten pitch [a residue of tar], and the liquors be stirred about alike to give them a vortical [rotating] motion; the pitch by its tenacity will lose its motion quickly, the oil being less tenacious will keep it longer, and the water being less tenacious will keep it longest, but yet will lose it in a short time. Whence it is easy to understand, that if many contiguous vortices of molten pitch were each of them as large as those which some suppose to revolve about the sun and fixed stars, yet these and all their parts would, by their tenacity and stiffness, communicate their motion to one another till they all rested among themselves. Vortices of oil or water, or some fluider matter, might continue longer in motion; but unless the matter were void of all tenacity and attrition of parts, and communication of motion (which is not to be supposed), the motion would constantly decay. Seeing therefore the variety of motion which we find in the world is always decreasing, there is a necessity of conserving and recruiting it by active principles, such as are the cause of gravity, by which planets and comets keep their motions in their orbits, and bodies acquire great motion in falling; and the cause of fermentation, by which the heart and blood of animals are kept in perpetual motion and heat; the inward parts of the earth are constantly warmed, and in some places grow very hot; bodies burn and shine, mountains take fire, the caverns of the earth are blown up, and the sun continues violently hot and lucid, and warms all things by its light. For we meet with very little motion in the world, besides what is owing to these active principles. And if it were not for these principles, the bodies of the earth, planets, comets, sun, and all things in them, would grow cold and freeze, and become inactive masses; and all putrefaction, generation, vegetation, and life would cease, and the planets and comets would not remain in their orbits.

All these things being considered, it seems probable to me, that God in the beginning formed matter in solid, massy, hard, impenetrable, moveable particles, of such sizes and figures, and with such other properties, and in such proportion to space, as most conduced to the end for which he formed them; and that these primitive particles being solids, are incomparably harder than any porous bodies compounded of them; even so very hard, as never to wear or break in pieces: no ordinary power being able to divide what God himself made one in the first creation. While the particles continue entire, they may compose bodies of one and the same nature and texture in all ages: but should they wear away, or break in pieces, the nature of things depending on them, would be changed. Water and earth, composed of old worn particles and fragments of particles, would not be of the same nature and texture now, with water and earth composed of entire particles in the beginning. And therefore, that nature may be lasting, the changes of corporeal things are to be placed only in the various separations and new associations and motions of these permanent particles; compound bodies being apt to break, not in the midst of solid particles, but where those particles are laid together, and only touch in a few points.

It seems to me farther, that these particles have not only a *vis inertiae*, accompanied with such passive laws of motion as naturally result from that force, but also that they are moved by certain active principles, such as is that of gravity, and that which causes fermentation, and the cohesion of bodies. These principles I consider, not as occult qualities, supposed to result from the specific forms of things, but as general laws of nature, by which the things themselves are formed; their truth appearing to us by phenomena, though their causes be not yet discovered. For these are manifest qualities, and their causes only are occult. And the Aristotelians gave the name of occult qualities, not to manifest qualities, but to such qualities only as they supposed to lie hid in bodies, and to be the unknown causes of manifest effects: such as would be the causes of gravity, and of magnetic and electric attractions, and of fermentations, if we should suppose that these forces or actions arose from qualities unknown to us, and incapable of being discovered and made manifest. Such occult qualities put a stop to the improvement of natural philosophy, and therefore of late years have been rejected. To tell us that every species of things is endowed with an occult specific quality by which it acts and produces manifest effects, is to tell us nothing: but to derive two or three general principles of motion from phenomena, and afterwards to tell us how the properties and actions of all corporeal things follow from those manifest principles, would be a very great step in philosophy, though the causes of those principles were not yet discovered: and therefore I scruple not to propose the principles of motion above mentioned, they being of very general extent, and leave their causes to be found out.

Now by the help of these principles, all material things seem to have been composed of the hard and solid particles above mentioned, variously associated in the first creation by the counsel of an intelligent agent. For it became him who created them to set them in order. And if he did so, it's unphilosophical to seek for any other origin of the world, or to pretend that it might arise out of a chaos by the mere laws of nature; though being once formed, it may continue by those laws for many ages. For while comets move in very eccentric orbits in all manner of positions, blind fate could never make all the planets move one and the same way in orbits concentric, some inconsiderable irregularities excepted, which may have risen from the mutual actions of comets and planets upon one another, and which will be apt to increase, till this system wants a reformation. Such a wonderful uniformity in the planetary system must be allowed the effect of choice. And so must the uniformity in the bodies of animals, they having generally a right and a left side shaped alike, and on either side of their bodies two legs behind, and either two arms, or two legs, or two wings before upon their shoulders, and between their shoulders a neck running down into a backbone, and a head upon it; and in the head two ears, two eyes, a nose, a mouth, and a tongue, alike situated. Also the first contrivance of those very artificial parts of animals, the eyes, ears, brain, muscles, heart, lungs, midriff, glands, larynx, hands, wings, swimming bladders, natural spectacles, and other organs of sense and motion; and the instinct of brutes and insects, can be the effect of nothing else than the wisdom and skill of a powerful ever-living agent, who being in all places, is more able by his will to move the bodies within his boundless uniform sensorium,[7] and thereby to form and reform the parts of the universe, than we are by our will to move the parts of our own bodies. And yet we are not to consider the world as the body of God, or the several parts thereof, as the parts of God. He is a uniform being, void of any members or parts, and they are his creatures subordinate to him, and subservient to his will; and he is no more the soul of them, than the soul of man is the soul of the species of things carried through the organs of sense into the place of its sensation, where it perceives them by means of its immediate presence, without the intervention of any third thing. The organs of sense are not for enabling the soul to perceive the species of things in its sensorium, but only for conveying them thither; and God has no need of such organs,

---

7 See n. 4 above.

he being everywhere present to the things themselves. And since space is divisible *in infinitum*, and matter is not necessarily in all places, it may be also allowed that God is able to create particles of matter of several sizes and figures, and in several proportions to space, and perhaps of different densities and forces, and thereby to vary the laws of nature, and make worlds of several sorts in several parts of the universe. At least, I see nothing of contradiction in all this.

As in mathematics, so in natural philosophy, the investigation of difficult things by the method of analysis, ought ever to precede the method of composition. This analysis consists in making experiments and observations, and in drawing general conclusions from them by induction, and admitting of no objections against the conclusions, but such as are taken from experiments, or other certain truths. For hypotheses are not to be regarded in experimental philosophy. And although the arguing from experiments and observations by induction be no demonstration of general conclusions; yet it is the best way of arguing which the nature of things admits of, and may be looked upon as so much the stronger, by how much the induction is more general. And if no exception occurs from phenomena, the conclusion may be pronounced generally. But if at any time afterwards any exception shall occur from experiments, it may then begin to be pronounced with such exceptions as occur. By this way of analysis we may proceed from compounds to ingredients, and from motions to the forces producing them; and in general, from effects to their causes, and from particular causes to more general ones, till the argument end in the most general. This is the method of analysis, and the synthesis consists in assuming the causes discovered, and established as principles, and by them explaining the phenomena proceeding from them, and proving the explanations.

In the two first books of these Opticks, I proceeded by this analysis to discover and prove the original differences of the rays of light in respect of refrangibility, reflexibility, and colour, and their alternate *fits of easy reflexion* and *easy transmission*, and the properties of bodies, both opaque and pellucid [transparent], on which their reflexions and colours depend. And these discoveries being proved, [they] may be assumed in the method of composition for explaining the phenomena arising from them: an instance of which method I gave in the end of the first book. In this third book I have only begun the analysis of what remains to be discovered about light and its effects upon the frame of nature, hinting several things about it, and leaving the hints to be examined and improved by the farther experiments and observations of such as are inquisitive. And if natural philosophy in all its parts, by pursuing this method, shall at length be perfected, the bounds of moral philosophy will be also enlarged. For so far as we can know by natural philosophy what is the first cause, what power he has over us, and what benefits we receive from him, so far our duty towards him, as well as that towards one another, will appear to us by the light of nature. And no doubt, if the worship of false gods had not blinded the heathen, their moral philosophy would have gone farther than to the four cardinal virtues; and instead of teaching the transmigration of souls, and to worship the sun and moon, and dead heroes, they would have taught us to worship our true author and benefactor, as their ancestors did under the government of Noah and his sons before they corrupted themselves.

Finis.

Index

CAMBRIDGE TEXTS IN THE HISTORY OF PHILOSOPHY

Titles published in the series thus far

3369456